The Alpine House
Its Plants and Purposes

The Rock Gardener's Library also includes:

A Manual of Alpine and Rock Garden Plants
Edited by Christopher Grey-Wilson

A Guide to Rock Gardening
Richard Bird

Forthcoming:

Gardening with Raised Beds and Tufa
Duncan Lowe

The Propagation of Alpine Plants and Dwarf Bulbs
Brian Halliwell

Alpines in the Open Garden
Jack Elliott

Robert Rolfe

The Alpine House
Its Plants and Purposes

CHRISTOPHER HELM
A & C BLACK · London

TIMBER PRESS
Portland, Oregon

© 1990 Robert Rolfe

Line illustrations by David Henderson

First published 1990 by Christopher Helm (Publishers) Ltd,
Imperial House, 21–25 North Street, Bromley, Kent BR1 1SD,
a subsidiary of A & C Black (Publishers) Ltd,
35 Bedford Row, London WC1R 4JH

ISBN 0–7136–8074–1

A CIP catalogue record for this book is available from the British
Library

First published in North America in 1990 by
Timber Press
9999 SW Wilshire
Portland, Oregon, 97225
USA

ISBN 0–88192–185–8

Typeset by Paston Press, Loddon, Norfolk
Printed and bound in Great Britain by The Bath Press

Contents

CONTENTS

Colour Plates

Figures

Introduction

For as long as the cultivation of alpine plants has been a significant activity, the need to imitate certain conditions of their natural environment has been apparent. Almost any rule has its exceptions, and it would be easy to sidetrack and consider the various ways in which alpines differ in their requirements. Broadly speaking, however, to cultivate them to an acceptable standard requires that we provide them with a well-drained compost where the available plant foods are released slowly, which is not quite the same as starving them altogether. The nitrogen content in particular is kept on the low side, for plants of the high screes often grow in soil of almost exclusively mineral content, where phosphorous, potassium and a string of trace elements provide the necessary nutrients.

Low temperatures in themselves are not usually a problem, but their timing can be, especially the late frosts that mark the start of the lowland growing season in many regions. And because snow cover cannot normally be guaranteed, nor the constant dormancy of the plants in winter be expected in a stop/start climate, it is quite possible to have plants die in a severe winter, even if we banish altogether the many dwarf plants of non-alpine origin that hover on the borderline of hardiness.

More damaging is an excess of moisture when the plants have ceased to make vegetative growth. The ground in which they grow can be raised above the general level, and water channelled away from their often vulnerable rootstocks by means of a coarse gravel topdressing, but there still remain many that prefer their foliage to remain dry under lowland conditions. Certain alpines that inhabit cliff overhangs or areas where evaporation rates are high enough to remove surface water within a matter of hours may object to overhead moisture at any time of the year.

Light levels also need consideration. One of the main challenges in growing alpines away from their native habitats is to reproduce the tightness of form and condensed appearance that frequently characterise healthy plants in the wild. Poor light is one significant reason why cultivated plants may forsake this habit and is a factor in the sparse flowering of some alpines in our gardens.

Finally, when they do flower, it is not always at a time when viewing them in the open garden could be thought of as pleasant. This may equally apply in their native mountains, be they the Himalayas at the height of the monsoon, the central Andes in the wet season or even the Alps in the midst of a blizzard. In the garden, flowering at a time of inclement weather can be a marked disadvantage, not only from the aesthetic point of view: it may hamper pollination and the setting of seed.

Much can be achieved in the open garden, and the number of alpines that will thrive outside is certainly far greater than people have until quite recently acknowledged. But even given piecemeal winter cover, extra efficient drainage and well-judged planting positions some alpines will not tolerate the local climate in all its phases. We want a means of growing them that promises their general health and long-term existence in our gardens, and also of studying them in the often difficult first years after their introduction to assess their likely needs.

The alpine house, which in one form or another has been with us for over a century (Kew's original model was built back in 1887) has always been associated with the cultivation of the more difficult alpines, by which is meant those that we maltreat by growing them under unsuitable conditions, often in ignorance of their growth cycle and general ecology. Periodically, the alpine house has come in for criticism based on our continued inability to cultivate certain alpines, and a belief that plants within its confines are protected from the very elements that have brought about the resilient, dwarfed characteristics associated with them. This is a half-truth, for the number of quite outstanding exhibits to be seen at specialist shows and in the collections of enthusiasts demonstrates what can be achieved, and as for failure, well, this is perhaps to be expected in a collection where so much of the material is unfamiliar, and advances achieved on the basis of trial and error.

Such experiments do not always filter down into popular usage, and it is still unusual to see features such as supplementary lighting, refrigerated benching and the dehumidifying units sold for domestic use, although all can assist in the cultivation of otherwise intractable alpines. None are indispensable, and much can be achieved using nothing more than a well-constructed, amply ventilated greenhouse that admits a high level of light and relies on restricted winter 'heating' only as a last ditch back up, which seems to sum up the alpine house as presently conceived.

It should not be thought that professional alpine growers hold the monopoly on innovations in this area, for it is frequently the specialist, concentrating on a small genus or very specific group, whose practical experiences bring about a change in the way we go about growing whatever alpine plant happens to be involved. Rather, there is an increasingly apparent interchange both of material and ideas between the two bodies, and this redounds to the general benefit of those interested in alpine house cultivation.

The decision on which plants to retain under the glass throughout the year, which to protect only in the winter or when at rest, and for that matter which to debar, must be left to the individual. He will take his cue from the prevailing climate, though always in conjunction with an awareness of the plants that experience has shown will thrive best in the alpine house, whether gardening in Birmingham, Alabama or Birmingham, England or indeed any of the many countries north and south of the Equator where alpine gardeners are to be found.

1 Suitability

Since the alpine house first appeared on the scene, critics have grumbled that many of its occupants are not alpines at all. What is sometimes forgotten is the corollary of this statement: not all alpines make suitable alpine house plants. Plants have their preferences, and a pot in a well-ventilated glasshouse can prove a hostile environment for a whole range of 'true' alpines.

Size and spread

Alpine plants are commonly said to be diminutive, but a visit to the mountains soon compromises this notion. Read back through the annals of the great plant collectors in the Himalayas and you will find reference to mats of cassiopes several metres across, the plants blending to form a continuous carpet much like heather on a Scottish moor. *Paraquilegia anemonoides* as received from the nurseryman presents itself as a slight and delicate tuft of glaucous, fern-like foliage in a 6cm pot, but Ludlow and Sherriff witnessed the same plant growing on the borderland between Tibet and Bhutan, and estimated many of the specimens to be 60cms across. *Haastia pulvinaris* is occasionally seen in specialist collections as a compact, densely hairy cushion, but on the consolidated screes of South Island, New Zealand, massive mounds extending to three metres are recorded; appropriately it is popularly referred to as the 'giant vegetable sheep'. So all things are relative. The interesting point is the length of time such plants take to grow to such a size. Many of the subshrubs develop woody trunks the width of a man's arm or more, and counting the rings through a cross section, much as a dendrologist would calculate the age of a tree, shows that such plants can be exceptionally long-lived, taking a century or more to attain their remarkable dimensions.

In these cases, the plants are frequently native to spartan environments, where the seed crop can fail, not just one year but several in succession, and such longevity is an essential mechanism to withstand the fallow years. Their rate of growth is too slow to present the gardener with a problem of accommodation in the short term. A principal reason for such plants not growing to similar dimension in cultivation is lack of space or a suitable receptacle in which to grow the steadily extending specimen.

Not all plants can be said to increase steadily, and it would be possible to list a host of plants that perhaps do not flourish outdoors, but spread so rampantly under glass that neighbouring plants are likely to be swamped in a matter of a few months, or sometimes weeks. *Pratia pedunculata* is a notorious example from the recent past, thought (because it was introduced from Australia and Tasmania) to be on the borderline of hardiness when it was first introduced to Britain in the 1970s, whereas nowadays the vigorous mats smothered in the summer with blue lobelia flowers, lovely though they may be, are viewed somewhat apprehensively by experienced gardeners. Many books recommend the rather similar, white flowered *Pratia angulata* as suitable for the alpine house, yet here we have a plant that can cover several metres of moist, peaty ground in a very few years, dying out at the centre if the peripheral runners are not laboriously trimmed away. Unless blessed with a glasshouse of the size normally associated with market gardens, the choice lies between annual propagation and replanting, or risking the possibility that a severe winter will dispose of outdoor colonies.

Very rarely, the vertical scale of a plant can cause some misgivings: at over 3,000m in the mountains of equatorial Africa, senecios up to 6m high thrive in a climate alternating between intense sunshine and dense freezing mists, and at similar latitudes in the Andes of Venezuela, Colombia and Ecuador, the genus *Espeletia* provides over 70 species which form attractive furry rosettes carried on even taller stalks that are coated with an insulation of dead leaves. Seed of these plants germinates well, and several of the espeletias have grown far better than might be expected in their early years, but they are unlikely to adapt well to the open garden, and their monumental scale does not accord with the majority of an alpine plant collection.

This dilemma will affect only a handful of gardeners, but the question of where to site plants whose leaves expand greatly after flowering is over has to be faced repeatedly. Nature orders things better: scree dwellers do not necessarily grow in isolation, but their growth rates are often similar and it is possible to find examples of one plant seeding into the mat of another, with the two growing happily together for a number of years. Lower down in the alpine meadows, growth is much lusher and the plants cram together, with ten or more species inhabiting a square metre by no means unusual. But the two growth types almost never mix, whereas in the alpine house a more cosmopolitan mix is artificially maintained. *Jeffersonia dubia* is repeatedly suggested as a good alpine house plant, and for the two or three days that its delicate lavender flowers hold intact above the crimson of the freshly emerging foliage this is undoubtedly true. As the last petals fall, however, the leaves are already burying the spent flowerheads, and within a few weeks an established clump can quite easily cover a metre or more with its lily-pad shaped leaves, although the dormant crown is probably less than a tenth of this distance across. The cover is so dense that, grown on the peat bed, self-sown seedlings will establish only beyond the perimeter of the canopy. Tucked away in a corner of the alpine house, the damage may not be apparent until the foliage dies away in the autumn to reveal a surround of smothered, vacant pots.

2 The structure and its siting

Alpine plants have been grown to a high standard in glasshouses sited in the most unlikely spots. A lean-to model, for example, can be successful if the plants have their pots turned to balance the growth in the one-directional light (up to once a week) and a north-facing position is avoided. Not everyone has the good fortune to be able to choose an ideal site, and some people will put the needs of the plants on a secondary footing, considering that the general look of the garden is more important, and placing the alpine house behind a screen, or at least away from the main vistas.

Even if starting off with a small alpine house, it is wise to leave room for an extension to be added on later, or for a second to take the overflow of plants that is the common lot of nearly every alpine gardener. It also helps if the frames and plunge beds that invariably accompany an alpine house can be positioned nearby, staggering halfway down the garden with a heavy pot being once of the less rewarding aspects of the hobby. It make sense to site the house adjacent to the dwelling, especially if supplies of electricity and water are likely to be required. More rarely, this proximity is made necessary for security purposes. There are many tales, not all of them apocryphal, of vandalism and plants that 'disappear'.

It has become standard practice to recommend that all greenhouses are orientated east–west to take advantage of increased light in the winter, but what is now always added is that with the smaller sizes there is almost no advantage in this positioning. More important is the avoidance of any deep shade likely to be cast by surrounding features, although the more delicate, transient shade provided by distant foliage can be a decided help in blocking the meridian sun and keeping the summer temperature down to a more reasonable level. Sometimes it is suggested that poor light levels in the winter are in part beneficial, helping to keep the temperature at a lower level, but in many areas the ambient temperature is regularly high enough to allow growth to proceed.

Legal considerations are unlikely to weigh very heavily, but in England affixing any structure to a dwelling requires planning permission, whilst where the land is not owned freehold, to fix the alpine house to a permanent base makes it the property of the landowner, not the tenant or person leasing the land.

The base itself must rest on a perfectly level site, and it is equally important to be sure that it will remain so, which in turn means that the subsoil should be firm. For preference, the alpine house must rest on a solid foundation, and if the land is in any way unsuitable it is worth obtaining a large set square and spirit level before laying down a course of brickwork – such a firm foundation is of greatest importance in very exposed positions, where the stability of the structure is otherwise imperiled. The majority of manufacturers can supply ready-made bases in various materials – precast concrete and steel being the normal choices – to which the main structure is simply bolted on. Any unevenness at the base will cause an eventual stress on the framework and if this is allowed to continue can result in gaps developing which bring with them rainwater which drips onto the plants below.

Originally, the alpine house was predominantly built as a solid-sided con-struction, using either brick or less regularly, timber. Both types are still in use to the present day, but since the nineteenth century the design of greenhouses has been radically changed and aluminium frame models, which require relatively little maintenance and are light yet strong, have been adopted as the most popular choice, partly on the grounds of cost but equally because the light is not blocked by a heavy framework.

Purpose-built alpine houses can still be obtained in western red cedar and (more rarely) brick based designs, and apart from their more pleasing appear-ance have some decided advantages. Specifically, cedar has properties of thermal insulation superior to aluminium (where heat is transmitted more quickly) which means that a more even temperature can be maintained, and condensation problems are less apparent. But if weather-boarding or brick is continuous to bench height, the chance to grow plants on a lower tier of staging has to be largely passed up. Moreover, a wooden framework will require regular painting with a preservative and the amount of light entering is somewhat reduced by the thicker glazing bars and general construction, timber being less strong than aluminium. Timber-frame glasshouses are usually easier to construct since they come in complete sections, perhaps even preglazed, whereas aluminium models invariably arrive in a series of long boxes, with the glass coming separately via a local glazier. Some firms offer a package deal and will contact a local builder to assemble the maze of pieces and in the United Kingdom, where this arrangement means that VAT taxation can be deducted, the overall price is little affected by this extra service.

As previously stated, the area chosen should be level, not susceptible to waterlogging (a tile drain may be necessary) and where possible away from the foot of a slope or hollow where cold air will accumulate to give a frost pocket. An exposed position, whilst allowing maximum light, can bring with it the likelihood of storm damage in areas where severe gales are experienced, but a solidly built glasshouse is surprisingly resilient in the face of such conditions, and damage is more likely to result from tree branches and other loose material crashing through the panes than the buffeting effect of the wind in itself.

The nature of the flooring material will be partly influenced by the decision of whether to use the area either side of the path as extra growing space. The most popular arrangement is to construct a central walkway of paving slabs, placing them on a 15cm-deep base of rubble and bedding then in builders sand, covering the remaining area with gravel or constructing plunge beds the length of the alpine house, which can be used to house plants undergoing a resting period and, if the light available is good enough, the overspill from the main benches. Alternatively the site can be concreted over, which gives an even surface and a firm foundation for the benching, and can be hosed down in hot weather to provide cooler conditions.

The staging

On rare occasions one sees an alpine house where the plants are grown in plunge beds at ground level, or even left free-standing on matting which is watered by means of a perforated hose. A more effective use of space requires the provision of benching, often with an understorey that proves handy for plants undergoing a resting period and those few plants (*Pleione*, for example) that grow well even in the less well-lit areas. The siting of the alpine house will influence what can be grown at the lower level – on open land where the glazing extends to the ground it can be utilised much in the same way as the upper tier, and the author has seen plants that object to poor light such as *Androsace delavayi* growing very well tucked away in a draughty corner since no space was available on the top bench to accommodate them.

The standard arrangement is to run a parallel set of benches either side of a central pathway, the crosspiece at one end frequently being omitted to allow for a second door, which helps greatly with ventilation. Really wide green-houses may be equipped with a third central bench, but this is far from common. Should the decision be made to construct the staging without relying on the several kitforms designed for the purpose, then the most important point to remember is that it will have to bear a very heavy weight, and concrete slabs, or well-seasoned timber supplied with cross-battens and leg braces, are generally superior to galvanised iron or corrugated asbestos, the keeping qualities of which are debatable. Some enthusiasts go one better and build a version of the brick-based plunge bed, which limits the range of plants that can be grown on the second tier, but provides excellent stability.

A comfortable working height approximates to waist level – commercial models are offered at anything from 69 to 92cm and similarly for ease of access the standard widths seldom exceed 90cm, with a rather cautious suggestion of half this figure for a standard 1.8m-wide alpine house. Whether a gap should be left between the benching and the glazing is a moot point: certainly this is not part of the design of the traditional alpine house where the plunge runs right up to the open windows or ventilators. Since cooler air sinks until it meets the benches, and is distributed over them, there is sound reasoning in continuing this arrangement. If the ventilators are below bench height, however, their effect will be largely lost.

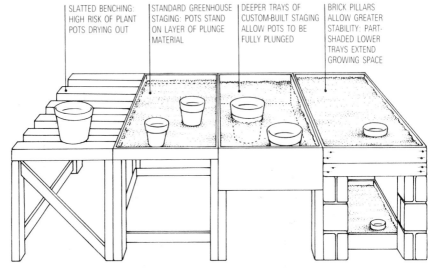

SLATTED BENCHING:
HIGH RISK OF PLANT
POTS DRYING OUT

STANDARD GREENHOUSE
STAGING: POTS STAND
ON LAYER OF PLUNGE
MATERIAL

DEEPER TRAYS OF
CUSTOM-BUILT STAGING
ALLOW POTS TO BE
FULLY PLUNGED

BRICK PILLARS
ALLOW GREATER
STABILITY: PART-
SHADED LOWER
TRAYS EXTEND
GROWING SPACE

Figure 1   The staging

The flooring too should be firm enough to support the weight, and a concrete base is usually best. The manufacturers of some brands of aluminium staging provide small footplates to help arrest the progressive sinking of the staging into softer surfaces, but these are unlikely to solve the problem completely.

Slatted staging has its adherents, and admittedly gives good air circulation, but the corollary of this is that the exposed pots dry out very quickly, and unless the owner is retired or can otherwise guarantee regular visits to the alpine house, the system as it stands is quite unworkable. It can, however, be adopted somewhat, using a series of shallow trays balanced on top and filled with a plunge material, which guarantees a better chance of survival.

A stronger construction, based on the same 'table top' design makes use of modular aluminium units, which can be added to in a variety of combinations to make best use of the space available, and are supported by tubular or angle aluminium legs, braced each corner with a flat bar, and open with a lower cross-bar to give added rigidity, on which a second series of trays can be placed. The trays are not necessarily deep (approx 2cm) but are generally covered with fine gravel or capillary matting, standing rather than burying the pots on this surfacing, and in the former instance watering on an individual basis, checking each pot and regulating the amount as required. If it proves difficult to apply water without wetting the foliage of a plant likely to resent such treatment, then the soak tray is utilised, but on the whole a small watering can with a long spout directed at the edge of the pot will prove satisfactory. Some designs incorporate trays that are purposely not enclosed at their corners, the intention being to let excess water drain away if they are flooded. Aluminium lacks the insulating properties of wood and frequently a liner is used to buffer the temperature variation that occurs diurnally.

This design can be modified to incorporate deeper trays, with sides some 15cm high allowing the pots to be plunged to a depth which accommodates all but the very largest sizes. Apart from providing a cooler root run and helping to minimise the risk of drying out, the plunge supports the pots and as such help to regularise the respective levels of the various sizes. Unplunged, it becomes necessary to group them together according to depth, if the smaller sizes are not to be overshadowed. The plunge material also helps to insulate against freezing of the roots in cold weather, and although open slatted staging provides better ventilated conditions at this time of the year, the advantage gained is offset by the vulnerability of the plants to frost drought, and the risk of failing to judge the moisture level of any one pot accurately, whereas by keeping the sand plunge just moist, little supplementary watering of the pots will be necessary until late winter.

Wood – deal and cedarwood are the standard choices – can be fashioned into trays of whatever depth is required by the handyman, and if treated with a preservative on a regular basis (assuming the fumes are not phytotoxic) will endure well. I have seen staging still in use after over 20 years, particularly if a polythene lining is incorporated, perhaps using a double thickness which finishes slightly higher than the uppermost level of the plunge material. Crosspieces at intervals upwards of a metre will help materially in the stability of the finished bench, and serve to counteract the bowing tendency caused by the weight of the moist sand.

'Sand' is here used interchangeably with plunge material, since it is superior in its ability to exert a drainage pull on the compost to other materials. It also holds its shape well when moist, which means that a pot can be taken away, examined, and returned without the need for re-excavation – something that is

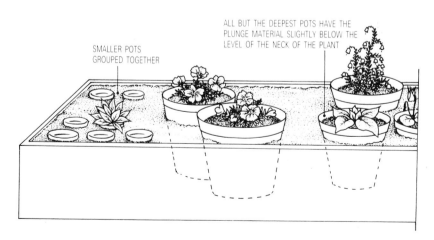

SMALLER POTS
GROUPED TOGETHER

ALL BUT THE DEEPEST POTS HAVE THE
PLUNGE MATERIAL SLIGHTLY BELOW THE
LEVEL OF THE NECK OF THE PLANT

Figure 2   Bench arrangement

difficult to effect if the pots surrounding the caved-in hole are packed closely together. Although sterile, it is surprising how quickly it becomes covered in algae, mosses and, not infrequently, seedlings that arise where part of the harvest escapes the gardener.

It is perhaps for this reason that other materials are sometimes utilised – fine granite chippings and pea gravel along with granulated clay products are the evident alternatives, but these are more in the nature of surfaces to stand the pots upon than to use at any great depth. Normally, the sand plunge comes to within 2–4 cm of the rim of the pot, although providing that over half the pot is buried, the exact depth is probably not critical.

Associated structures

Owning an alpine house is all very well, but the conditions it provides are not always flexible enough to cope with the needs of the plants that it shelters, nor is it likely as the collection expands that there will be enough room to retain all its occupants the year round. In the majority of cases, it exists not only to grow the plants but equally to display them, and once the period of peak interest for a particular species has passed, it may be more appropriate (and possibly advantageous for subsequent growth) to move it elsewhere and make way for an ever-changing succession of plants.

The degree of rotation will depend not only on the particular interests of the gardener but even more upon his or her energy, for it can be a time-consuming process and, when considering the larger pot sizes, almost a trial of strength. The local climate will influence the choice of candidates: in the drier eastern counties of England, for instance, even species of *Eriogonum* from semi-desert habitats can be placed out of doors in the summer, whereas in areas of higher summer rainfall they usually collapse, no matter how well drained the compost, and do not compare in appearance with year-round occupants of the alpine house.

There is much to be said for keeping a 'backbone' range of plants to bring interest to the alpine house after the main flowering trails off. Some belong to this category but retain their place by virtue of their attractive foliage – *Convolvulus boissieri* (Plate 13) can be grown outside, but makes an excellent potplant, whilst the tight silver huddles of *Lupinus lepidus* v. *lobbii* are always worthy of a second look, assuming that the parallel interest of the red spider mite can be restrained.

What sorts out those that stay from those that are moved is often their tolerance of heat, for the strictly air-conditioned environment that has been provided by some institutions in the USA and elsewhere is still beyond the resources of most amateurs. Only so much can be done to control the glasshouse temperature in the summertime, and it may not be enough to mollify plants used to monsoon conditions in the growing period, or a nightly cooling period during which the temperature drops sharply, so different from the unremitting warmth or muggy heat of some lowland summers.

10

It is, unsurprisingly, plants from the drier mountain ranges that adjust best to a summer in the alpine house – most species of *Dionysia*, the woolly leaved Drabas, *Primula allionii*, *Gilia caespitosa* and so on. Of the others, some are only brought into the alpine house so that their flowers can be appreciated, some needed a cooler (not necessarily moist) summer rest, and some dislike winter wet, but are happy in the open garden until their winter semi-resting state takes hold in October/November.

The most versatile system envisages both a cold frame and a plunge bed . . . the latter in effect the same as the alpine house bench, but open to the elements for the summer months. If space is available close to the alpine house, so much the better – it is customary to reserve the area along one or both sides for this purpose, but it may also be necessary to select a more shaded area, near a boundary hedge for instance, if woodland species such as *Epigaea gaultherioides* or some of the Petiolarid primulas and *Cyclamen* are being grown.

The traditional alpine house, being brick based, was often abutted with a continuous cold frame built in the same material, the succession of lights sometimes hinged at the wall side and sloping down to the lower front edge where they were lifted open to be secured on ratching. Alternatively, the lights were simply rested on the framework (requiring them to be lashed down with cabling against winter storms) and removed altogether in fine weather, or propped open if overhead moisture needed to be excluded. Ventilation was not particularly efficient, nor was light distribution ideal.

Also still available are wooden frames, again single span, usually with two dutch lights that slide backwards along a central T-shaped bar, which is echoed either side by a wooden channel at the same level. The further the framelight is pulled back, the more air is admitted, but obviously once more than half is suspended behind, the likelihood is that the weight will tilt it backwards and send it crashing to the ground. Some models have an upper guiding track, so that the edge of the light is enclosed above and below, but my experience has been that after a year or two, the weight of the light prizes off the roof of the channel. If plants requiring protection from overhead moisture are grown, it is wiser to grow them towards the back rather than get caught out when a thunderstorm breaks and the front portion of the frame is soaked. This touches on another disadvantage; unless the lights are closed down, then water streams down the tilted glass, overflows the narrow wooden lip that holds the glass in place, and spills with force onto whatever lies underneath. Opening and shutting the frames – even if the lights are removed in the summer and it is only spread over a three month period – can wear down the most patient of individuals. Two further considerations: the level of humidity is likely to remain high because the sides are enclosed (the frame is really just a slanting box with a lid) and although light within can be improved by painting the inside white to increase the amount reflected, this type of cold frame still provides a less well-lit environment than the average alpine house. This may well be advantageous for plants such as *Ramonda myconi* and the woodland species of

Trillium, but is of less use when attempting plants from draughty environments that are accustomed to high light levels.

Nowadays, these problems are overcome by lightweight aluminium structures, available both in lean-to and span designs, that are much akin to miniature greenhouses. Rather than having lights to protect and hold the glass in place, they are fitted with standard size panes of horticultural glass which overlap one another, and can be slid across another to provide controlled ventilation over any specified part of the frame. Rainwater is channelled along the roof edges and drains away through a break in the metal at either end. This makes it possible to leave the roofing glass sections in place but remove all the side panels of glass on the leeward side unless snow flurries are anticipated. The opposite panels can be repositioned, i.e. doubled up during the daytime, so that air blows across the plants, and in summertime it may prove advantageous to remove *all* the glass, leaving the structure in place so that shading material can be strung across if necessary.

Several heights can be chosen, a ridge height of 45cm being satisfactory for the vast majority of alpines, although the taller Oncocyclus irises and shrubs such as *Daphne jezoensis* would be more comfortably housed in a 60cm high model (Plate 9). Apart from a side strut, no other vertical supports (a central post, for example) are incorporated in the design of the standard commercial models, which can be up to 3m long by 1.2m across.

Some people have found that heavy snow, particularly when followed by rain, can weigh down on the glass and cause it to collapse inwards; reports of the metal structure itself failing are infrequent. I have never experienced this, perhaps because on the rare occasions when more than 30cm of snow has fallen, I have always gone outside with a soft house brush and reduced the covering; but logically, since the glass is the same as that used in the alpine house, then if one gives so should the other.

The greatest problem has been separating the sliding panels when condensation has in effect glued them together. A thin flange along the exposed edges would help to provide a slight air gap between the overriding panels, and also protect fingers from the sharp edges. It is easy to let the end panel protrude beyond the structure, come round the corner five minutes later and walk straight into it. And if any gravel drops into the base channel unnoticed, the glass riding against it can fracture. All in all the occasional broken pane is to be expected by all but the most diligent owner.

Whilst the base can rest as constructed on a concrete standing or vacant piece of ground, it is preferable to raise it enough to allow for 30cm of plunge material, and perhaps to an even greater height if the owner objects to going down on all fours each time he or she wishes to retrieve a plant. Railway sleepers are sometimes used, but breeze blocks provide a more widely available alternative, though not a very sightly one. Better still are the engineering bricks or similarly shaped 'patio' bricks made of reconstituted stone, which can be interlocked, cemented together as if building a wall, and checked with a spirit level until the desired height is reached. Such a structure should last a lifetime. If the interior is lined with heavy-duty polythene to exclude soil pests, a drainage pipe will need to be inserted in the first course above ground level.

For anyone wanting a structure raised still further off the ground, a series of brick pillars supporting paving slabs that form the base of the plunge, building up the edge with two or three courses of bricks is pleasanter to look at than the angle iron structures that would look more at home in an engineering workshop. The final weight of the raised frame means that footings will be required if it is not to sink ignominiously after a couple of years.

Although we have talked of glass throughout, there is increasing use being made of rigid sheeting, which is lighter (and so needs to be anchored all the more effectively) but decidedly more expensive. Acrylic sheeting comes nearest to glass, whereas some of the film plastics have a much shorter life but are cheap enough to replace and can be pinned to simple wooden frames which are removed when the plants are in growth.

Some devotees construct a number of frames for specific purposes – in particular the housing of seed pots and the rearing of the young plants. The popularity of the 'cuttings frame' however, has waned, except perhaps in commercial establishments. Conversely, the pronounced increase in growing bulbous plants – considered as alpines even when their habitat might suggest otherwise – has inspired the rise of the bulb frame, where broadly speaking summer rainfall can be shielded and the winter moisture level controlled. Bulbs can be planted out, kept in their pots, or (more recently) planted in plastic lattice pots: the idea being that they appear to be growing in a glass covered border but can be lifted *in toto* and placed in a clay pot if required for exhibition or alpine house display. This can work well although stoloniferous species (some *Crocus*, for example) and generally those that make a lot of root growth (*Erythronium*, certain *Iris*) do not adapt very well.

Raised plunge beds are really frame bases without the covering, and are normally filled with builders' sand though this may need 'stirring' twice a year to keep down moss and liverwort growth or very fine grit. Check the pH, however, to be certain that the lime content is not excessive. The material needs to be finer than that which makes up the potting compost if it is to regulate the water content of the pots, supplying moisture by means of capillary action and draining the surplus.

Watering may be necessary on a daily basis in the summer if the bed is in an exposed position or the plants contained predominantly shallow rooted, but a watering can with a fine rose soon completes the process, whereas in the alpine house a less generalised approach is usually required.

3 Ventilation

The principal function of the various openings along the sides and roof of the alpine house is to provide a frequent exchange of air and to moderate the temperature. This is connected in most minds with one of the beneficial side effects, which is to lessen the humidity level. The standard greenhouse, it must be said, is inadequately ventilated, and it will be noticed that purpose-built alpine houses almost invariably have continuous ridge ventilation, with a further set of ventilators or windows, normally at bench height, running along either side. There is an obvious disparity between this arrangement and the 'two up, two down' roof lights and side sashes to be found in general-purpose models, but it is often possible for an extra payment to supplement the existing provisions.

With almost any greenhouse crop, it is estimated that an area of the framework corresponding to 20 per cent of the floor area should be given over to ventilators. Bearing in mind the windswept crannies and exposed screes favoured by numerous alpines, it will be seen that even this figure is on the conservative side. In practice, the door and side ventilators are left open in all but heavy frost, fog and driving rain. Additionally, it may prove beneficial temporarily to remove one or two panes of glass from the central end section if a second door is not already in place. How easy this will be depends on the original method of securing them: some are held in place with glazing clips alone and yield easily.

The natural ventilation of the alpine house can be supplemented by an electric fan. Some models can be purchased which double up as fan heater if necessary, but are chiefly used to stir the air and have a direct cooling effect if positioned so that the draught created blows over the benching. Siting the unit can prove awkward: if placed on the lower tier of benching and tilted upwards the full effect is not felt, but it is too bulky to fit on a bracket (unlike the household/ office fans also used that alter their direction backwards and forwards, describing a semi-circular pattern) and the exact positioning may be limited by the length of flex provided and the source of the power point. For the height of summer and on still, damp days throughout the year, it is advantageous to keep the unit running continuously, and the cost of doing so is modest.

The ridge lights will need opening or partially closing, depending on the likelihood of rain, for a heavy shower can play havoc if water falls on damp-intolerant cushions or dashes newly opened blooms. It is possible to fit auto-matic opening devices which are triggered by a rise or fall in temperature,

14

this in turn causing the expansion/contraction of either mineral wax or a metal alloy contained in a stainless steel tube which pushes a piston to open, and swings shut again as the wax contracts with a fall in temperature. Such units can be adjusted to operate when the air temperature exceeds 15°C and similar devices can be fitted to the side louvres.

However, manual control of the side louvres is normally quite adequate. A handle on the inside allows the pieces of glass (most louvres consist of five 'blades' of glass) to be tilted or moved to the horizontal position to admit air freely: for most of the year the latter position will be preferable. With benching that runs flush with the inner framework it is normal to position the louvres at bench height, but the more orthodox placement is lower down to foster the so-called 'chimney effect', whereby warm air rises and escapes through the ridge vents and is replaced by cooler air from outside entering at the base. In the summer, the alpine

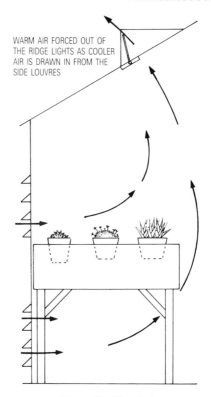

WARM AIR FORCED OUT OF THE RIDGE LIGHTS AS COOLER AIR IS DRAWN IN FROM THE SIDE LOUVRES

Figure 3   Ventilation

house interior will still be warmer than the outside, but the aim is to modulate the temperature to within a few degrees of the latter, and to achieve this cooling effect the floor is often damped down – i.e. hosed with water.

The need for efficient ventilation is apparent the year round, and whilst temperature control is particularly important in the summer, one should be aware that even in mid-winter sunshine can promote unseasonal warmth if the alpine house is left closed down – following a sharp frost, for instance.

During the resting period, condensation or damp air can soon give rise to the conditions under which fungal diseases thrive, and in the majority of gardens high humidity levels cause more problems during the winter than any other single factor. Fog and dense freezing mists are particularly awkward to cope with, and apart from installing an extractor fan, the best we can normally do is to avoid any watering whilst such conditions prevail, and try to counteract the effects by providing maximum ventilation in their wake, having closed everything down for their duration.

Attention paid to the initial siting of the alpine house will pay off at such times – as previously noted, frost pockets and hollows where damp air collects must be avoided if at all possible. On rare occasions ventilation may be too efficient, and gardeners living in areas prone to severe winter gales may need to plant a shelter screen of trees to filter the stronger gusts of the prevailing wind. It is better to leave the ventilators slightly open in a gale, although obviously the doors should be shut and secured.

The degree of ventilation is measured in terms of air changes per hour, and small glasshouses, where the temperature rises and falls with particular rapidity (as a result of the large surface to volume ratio) need proportionally more ventilation to bring about the same degree of cooling as in a large model. When the sun shines on glass, it raises the temperature far more quickly than the heat trapped inside can escape, and ventilation has to be considered as part of an equation to keep temperatures down, with shading and adequate watering also playing their part.

In general, it is preferable to provide too much rather than too little ventilation, the effects of high temperatures and close, damp conditions being more harmful to most alpine plants than wind scorch or drying out, which can be offset by keeping the pots in a sand plunge.

Temperament

Gardening under glass allows for considerable manipulation of the local climate, but the drier, warmer atmosphere is not liked by all alpines, just as the reduced light levels that result from summer shading (and before that, those light rays blocked by the untreated glass) can have an inimical effect. Merely bringing plants from high altitudes to lowland conditions has well-documented morphological consequences; some rather subtle – the concentration of stomata and the thickness of the cuticle, and others, such as the size of the leaf and its girth, more tangible. An interesting experiment carried out in 1948 by the Carnegie Institute of Washington, using several clones of *Achillea* species collected at varying altitudes and grown at high, low and intermediate stations, appeared to indicate that whilst the high altitude race would grow and indeed flower near to sea level, the plants were less vigorous and flowering sparser.

Any plant kept under permanently protected conditions is liable to be more 'open' than its toughened, weather-clipped equivalent growing in exposed conditions. What no one has yet explained satisfactorily is why some alpines can be persuaded to retain much of the same appearance that characterises them in the wild, whereas others (from the same habitat in some instances) need unremitting effort if they are to be grown to recapture their natural persona. We read of impossible plants but there are almost no alpines that someone somewhere has not managed to succeed with, if only for a short while. If the end result is an unhappy plant looking nothing like the robust wild version, however, then what is the point of the exercise?

An interesting illustration of this phenomenon occurs with the European Aretian androsaces, for whilst most can be grown to a high standard in the alpine house, *A. glacialis* (the highest occurring of all, seldom growing below 2,000m) nearly always forsakes the tight mats smothered in pink or white flowers that are the hallmark of the species on its exposed acidic screes. The rosette elongates and enlarges, leading to a loose cushion which flowers infrequently and begrudgingly. Better results are sometimes achieved by keeping the plant outdoors for the growth season, and the suggestion is that the lack of ultra violet light (which as generations of sunburned climbers could tell you, is far more intense at high altitudes) is largely responsible.

Temperature is likely to be another controlling factor: the androsace is generally found within easy distance of the permanent snow line, and even on a day of uninterrupted sunshine, temperatures ten or more degrees lower than in the village where your climb began are likely. This may explain why plants like *Ranunculus glacialis* are seldom successful under glass, for when they are found at lower altitudes, as for instance in Norway (where the species can stray from the high mountain screes that are its principal habitat in the Alps and Pyrenees), it is likely the effect of latitude provides a broadly similar climate.

What is not sufficiently appreciated, perhaps, is the multiplicity of ways in which plants that inhabit high altitudes have managed to survive the challenges of their environment. Sometimes, the leaves have a dense woolly covering of hairs that trap moisture – test this by blowing on the plant and you will notice that the moisture in your breath turns the leaves temporarily white as the mist is trapped like fog on a spider's web in the early morning. In the short growing season, there may not be time to develop much topgrowth, but even small seedlings frequently have a substantial root system. Owners of such plants sometimes worry that the apparently sluggish growth rate is indicative of something wrong with the growing conditions, and attempt to encourage a swifter response by supplementary feeding, a richer compost or the implementation of some misguided theory concerning an indispensable compost ingredient. That a larger plant may result is not in doubt, but bigger is not always better, and if a short-lived, atypically lax plant is created, then trying to regain an acceptable appearance can create more work and waste more time than the exercise of straightforward patience.

The first few years in a plant's lifetime, and especially the first season, may confuse the inexperienced, because repeatedly the manner of growth does not fully correspond to that of later life. Leaves may be larger than expected, flowering irregular or frugal, and the overall silhouette of the plant scarcely suggestive of the same species at maturity.

Plants from the high screes in many cases adapt to the instability of their homelands by sending out runners through the loose debris. These normally turn woody with age, the foliage at their very tips the only sign of life until the root system is traced back a metre or more along the resilient network of stolons. If shorn away when rock fragments dislodge and career down the mountainside, burying or scissoring all in their path, then a new rosette is formed close to the damaged stub, and frequently dormant growth buds further up the stem are stimulated. Such plants can look unkempt and 'straggly' under glass, and a combination of topdressing with coarse rock fragments and judicious pruning can pay dividends.

What cannot always be judged with certainty is whether seemingly etiolated growth is likely to compact with age as subsidiary shoots develop along the leader, or whether the plant in question is merely restrained when growing at the upper limit of its distribution, in which case it will revert to type in the absence of artificial inducements when grown at lower altitudes.

There is no one solution to the problem of persuading alpine plants to retain their characteristic appearances when brought into lowland cultivation. Taking just one example, *Androsace mucronifolia* flowers poorly for most people when brought into lowland cultivation. The rosettes may be several times the size of those formed at over 3,000m in the western Himalayas. By cultivating this species in a very lean compost and taking pains to counter the increased risk of drying out at the root, it has been possible to encourage compact growth and much better flowering. Applied to other genera where similar difficulties are experienced, this treatment might result in starvation – it is all a matter of educated guesswork.

One final observation: alpine gardeners may expect their charges to exhibit the hallmarks of good health the year round, but if they could be taken to see them growing in their natural habitats, some would have the shock of their lives. In regions where summer rainfall is uncertain and snowmelt does not always provide a reserve supply of moisture, the appearance of plants that would, under alpine house conditions, spend their summers green and turgid, is alarming. In the Balkans, the shrivelling of *Ramonda nathaliae* on its parched limestone cliff sites is a regular part of the annual cycle; so too is the way in which some *Dionysia* cushions 'dry up' in the heat of an Iranian summer until all but the centre of each rosette is khaki coloured, or the scree conditions of pulvinate *Phlox* in the mountains of Montana and Nevada. We may feel disinclined to subject our plants to the extremes that provoke such responses, but it is useful to remember that, once established, many plants are more tenacious than might be imagined.

Overhead moisture

It is very seldom that the alpine house provides enough room for all the plants that its owner wishes to grow, and soon after acquiring one, it becomes necessary to restrict the flow of new stock. There is more flexibility for anyone owning a cold frame or a raised bed, since the occupants can be changed depending on their stage of growth, but even the routine operations of repotting and propagating from existing material can very quickly inspire a review of which species really *need* protection at some stage.

The choice of plants will vary somewhat from district to district, for a species which thrives outside in coastal areas may not survive a winter further inland, but the preference is to include alpines which cannot be grown to a satisfactory standard in the owner's garden, and frequently those that have not been tried before, where the matter is yet in doubt.

The most obvious group of plants for inclusion are those that cannot cope with high rainfall during their dormant period, which in this context is taken as the time when foliar growth is minimal or non-existent. For most alpines, this is the period November–February, when the majority would be covered by snow. It should not be assumed that the plants are competely inert during these months – various cellular changes are taking place inperceptibly and in a changeable winter root growth will progress, though at a slow rate. But evaporation and transpiration will be at a minimum, and high alpines generally will resent any excess that does not drain or quickly dry away in the breeze.

Incidentally, there is no such thing as a consistent snowline in the mountains –something abundantly clear since package ski tours became popular, with hordes of holidaymakers scouring the lower slopes for a crisp and even covering in the middle of winter. This goes some way to explaining why many alpines can tolerate changeable lowland winters: conditions are not always predictable at home in the mountains either.

Glass does not insulate in the same way as a blanket of snow, nor do the light levels available to glasshouse plants match those to which dormant high alpines are subject, but although sophisticated techniques like refrigeration and controlled illumination are now within range of the enterprising amateur, the alpine house still provides a simple method of persuading a wide variety of plants to persist in alien climes.

Many bulbs from alpine regions appreciate the shedding of excess winter rainfall, and will need – in the majority of cases – a dry summer after the foliage dies away until root growth comes again, generally following a fall in night-time temperatures. There should be no wholehearted adoption of 'baking' (i.e. leaving the unplunged pots dry and exposed to all available sun under glass) since this can adversely affect the flowering of, for example, some species of *Fritillaria*, for which a plunge bed situated below the staging is far superior. Others, notably the more southerly occurring *Narcissus* and *Iris* belonging to the sections Regelia, Scorpiris and Oncocyclus are happier with higher soil temperatures – indeed a number of the latter are desert plants whose shallow-seated rhizomes must receive a substantial blessing of heat. Fieldwork carried out in the Elburz mountains of Iran (Mathew, *The Iris* 1982, p. 46) suggests that even in mid autumn the soil remains warm, and soon afterwards the plants are covered by snow.

A number of alpine plants are vulnerable to overhead moisture at almost any time of the year and, whilst the odd success is recorded with open ground plants, success is far more likely under glass. Nearly all are chasmophytic, which simply means that they grow on cliffs or, in an interesting variation of this theme, on the overhang of caves, where what little rainfall that blows onto them soon clears. In Europe, the best-known example is *Primula allionii*, hybrids of which will usually tolerate overhead watering whereas the species itself will more often than not suffer. The genus *Dionysia* is another group where the odd specimens grown on a raised bed for a few years do not compensate for the mass of corpses that have resulted from specimens experimentally planted, without overhead protection. Many species of *Draba* grow happily in the open, but the tomentose species such as *D. acaulis* and *D. mollissima* from Turkey and the Caucasus act as sponges and, if they live, hardly compare with those allocated alpine house space. The mountains of New Zealand are not universally shrouded in cloud, nor is rainfall exceptionally high outside the Westland ranges, which is why woollier species of *Raoulia* are kept under glass. Look in the floras and you will find that they come from dry, rocky places where the wind funnels between the rock outcrops, removing any surface water.

Similarly, flocculent plants are to be found all over the world, their representatives appearing spasmodically in the alpine houses of enthusiasts skilful enough to raise them from seed, for the very adaption that enables them to survive in their native mountains commonly signifies a marked reluctance to adapt to widescale cultivation.

Hardiness

Alpine gardeners are apt to quibble over the exact meaning of the word hardy, pointing out that several criteria are involved and that plants vary in their degree of tolerance from year to year, and from garden to garden. So they do, but it is broadly agreed that the term implies a plant able to withstand temperatures of 0°C or less in its winter resting period. Cold snaps that strike once growth is under way – June frosts and laggard snowfalls weighing on new shoots – are obviously damaging, as they are in the mountains. I have been in the Austrian Alps in mid-June when such conditions have damaged primulas and other 'hardy' plants that were in full flower when the weather changed.

Not only the severity but the duration of wintery conditions may be significant, for death can occur both by the well-documented process of the cell wall rupturing or by drought pure and simple. A plant on a well-drained slope whose roots extend a long way into a large mass of soil is manifestly better able to fend off adverse temperatures than one growing unplunged in a shallow pan. Equally, reading that the thermometer is registering −40°C in parts of the Alps does not mean that the plants will be enduring this degree of cold, for a snow covering several metres thick may be providing significant insulation. Nearly 30 years ago it was established (Ylimaki, 1962 in Woodward, *Climate and Plant Distribution* 1987) that deep snow cover could account for a difference between air and ground surface temperature of up to 30°C. Think of those survival courses where the recruits build a snow tunnel if the weather closes in.

In the alpine house, it is the later winter that causes most concern, for new shoots appear in some seasons as early as January, and once under way the plants have to be nursed through often rigorous conditions. An added difficulty is that cold water is viscous and cannot be taken up as easily by the roots, so that on a sunny day the leaves may be losing water but the plant unable to replace this loss at a comparable rate.

Most plants are prepared for winter temperatures by a change in day length, and various changes take place in the cells. The tissues, for instance, store more sugars and other soluble substances that serve to lower the freezing point and help prevent damage. This is not quite the case with plants from the tropics, where the climate is not so much seasonal as diurnal. Plants in active growth at midday are frozen solid a few hours later, which is significant since actively growing plant cells are usually more susceptible to frost damage. Elsewhere in the Himalayas, there are plants that may not experience any frosts at all – drenching rain when the monsoon comes, certainly, but the roots are snow covered when the temperature drops, and the growing season, though cool, is not characterised by excessively low night-time temperatures.

From here, it is a short step to those plants from the lower slopes that have to be maintained carefully when the temperature drops, and how inconsistent are our responses on this subject. Staying for a moment in the Himalayas, the epiphytic pleiones are widely viewed with suspicion, and admittedly they tend to occur at relatively modest elevations in the forests, but so too do many of the Petiolarid primulas whose alpine credentials are seldom questioned, notwithstanding the crippling effect of frost on the precocious flower buds. Similarly, in Europe, nearly all the species of *Cyclamen* are regarded as appropriate plants for the alpine house, yet very few are more than subalpine in distribution, and their resilience obliquely confirms the occasional harsh winter spells that interrupt a mediterranean climate.

What has to be remembered is that in bringing together plants from different zones that experience widely varying climatic conditions, we create a community that has no naturally occurring parallel. Most – if not all – alpines are able to prevent some amount of freezing injury, but the critical temperature varies widely, although a threshold of −15°C is a useful rule of thumb. Whilst some will happily tolerate considerably lower temperatures, experience has shown that prolonged exposure at such levels invariably leads to casualties.

Frost protection

Alpine gardeners sometimes take a perverse delight in cataloguing their losses after severe winter weather, and pride themselves on providing minimum protection, but there are several measures that can be taken to insulate plants when an especially cold spell is forecast. Even if you are not concerned for the health of the plants, it is worth remembering that frost can play havoc with clay flowerpots, not simply causing flaking of the rim but – by expansion of the compost as it freezes – completely shattering the body of the container.

The plants requiring most attention are those still in active growth, or that bloom during the winter months: these generally lack the toughened leaves and shoots characteristic of 'classic' alpines. If grown in a mixed collection, rather than accorded a separate glasshouse to themselves, then it is sensible to group them together, preferably plunged, since the roots will be taking up water unless the the compost is frozen, and the greater mass of the plunge material helps to protect against this.

Traditionally, gardeners have carefully placed unfolded sheets of newspaper

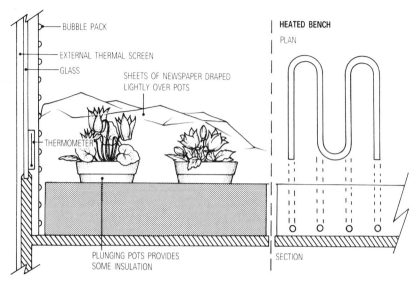

Figure 4   Methods of frost protection

over vulnerable plants, and this remains an effective insulator. A thickness of two or three sheets is ample – the aim is to trap air beneath the cover and prevent frost settling on the foliage. In the still conditions that prevail when a severe frost is experienced, this is a worthwhile practice, but searing cold easterly winds can play havoc with the arrangement, blowing the layers hither and thither. Another point worth noting is that the sheets have to be changed frequently; during the daytime the temperature may rise well above freezing point, and unless removed there is a danger of the absorbent paper coating the plants in a soggy wrapping.

More recently, it has become possible to purchase a thermal screen – a roll of insulating material that can be attached to the outside of the alpine house in much the same way that slatted blinds are anchored, except that ideally the screen should reach to the ground. Again, in areas that experience turbulent winds this advice needs modification, and here it is worthwhile buying lengths of bubble polythene (the material commonly used for packaging) that can be attached to the *inside* of the framework quite easily, and have not caused condensation problems when taken down as soon as the weather relents. This material is sold by the roll, and can be cut to size – as a rough guide a 1.8m × 2.4m greenhouse would require 36m of polythene sheeting 60cm wide (the standard measurement in which it is supplied) for complete insulation. To keep the sheeting in place, merely stretch pieces of cable or string from one end of the greenhouse to the other, both at the ridge and again at the eaves. Then thread the lengths between the restraints and the glass, perhaps affixing further by means of those locking devices that fit into the glazing channels of aluminium greenhouses. With a wooden greenhouse drawing pins perform the same function.

1. A typical upper scree slope in the Argentinian Andes

2. Excess moisture is often shed by virtue of the plant's windswept position

3. *Jankaea heldreichii* on Mount Olympus

4. The alpine house bench in mid-spring

5. A frame takes care of the overflow collection

These activities may seem time-consuming, but except in very cold districts (where the climate makes growing anything but the most cold-tolerant plants unrewarding anyway) such protection can be seen as an infrequent defence against unusually harsh weather. With truly alpine plants, very low temperatures more often cause damage than killing those in its grip outright, and it makes obvious sense to spend the odd hour ensuring against unnecessary disfigurement. The alternative might be several years wait until the frosted plant can be persuaded to regain its form.

Blowing hot and cold

Increasingly, alpine gardeners have accepted that *limited* use of artificial heat is beneficial, although there is still some disquiet over the precise degree of use. The need for restraint has not always been understood, except of course by the plants, which respond to frost-free conditions by out of season growth (often at the expense of flowers) that etiolates in the low winter light levels, or else produce their blooms over a period rather than surging into growth and flowering wholeheartedly.

However, for seedlings that germinate in late autumn, for recently cultivated material whose cold hardiness is not proven, for the many plants from mountainous areas that seldom achieve full dormancy under lowland conditions, a means of guarding against intense cold is worthwhile.

The most localised means makes use of soil warming cables, which can be purchased in kit form (varying lengths are available) together with a thermostatic control. This has a wide range of settings, but for our purposes the minimum temperature of 2°C should be adequate. The preferred method is to fill the tray with a layer of fine grit or coarse sand to a depth of some 5cm. The cabling is then placed on top in parallel lines, smoothly curved at the ends: any crossing will lead to overheating. A similar depth of plunge material is placed above, and the pot bases rested on this surface – alternatively 10–15 cm of material will ensure that the pots are plunged to a reasonable depth, and prevent the root area from freezing solid. Two points to bear in mind here: (1) root growth can be expected throughout the winter, so on balance the demand for water will be greater than with other occupants of the alpine house; (2) unless the pots are checked every few weeks, roots can quickly grow through the drainage holes and anchor securely in the plunge: severing them can be injurious to the plant. Some gardeners go further and place a plastic hood over the bench, held off the plants by several metal hoops, when severe frost is forecast, but this application is principally of use when attempting off-season cuttings, and the high humidity of the microclimate created is inimical to many alpines.

A wide range of greenhouse heaters can be found on the market, but few have great relevance to the alpine house, involving unnecessary expense and, all too often, creating more problems than they solve. The only appliance which will be considered here is the electric fan heater, which unlike the fixed

23

systems is simplicity to install, compact and versatile, and in some models doubles up to distribute cool air through the alpine house in the summer.

With some greenhouse crops, a precise winter minimum temperature must be maintained – any lower and the plants perish. The alpine gardener can afford a much more relaxed approach: the fan heater is a back-up system, which in some seasons might not be used at all, but will block the effects of a late season cold snap or make it possible to halt the damage caused by drought brought on by sustained frost. This is especially relevant if the plants are grown unplunged.

Depending on where the power point is situated, it may not be possible to be flexible in the choice of positioning for the unit, but to aid good overall distribution the far end of the alpine house, facing directly down the gangway, is a suitable site. Some types of benching come with a lower tier which provides a convenient shelf and does away with the likelihood of tripping over the heater whilst engrossed in attending to the plants.

Amateur models are usually designed to operate at 2,000 watts, and this power consumption should be expected to service a 3m × 2.4m greenhouse, which size encompasses the models used by the majority of gardeners. Although the units are normally provided with thermostatic control, it is unlikely that a setting lower than 0°C will be encountered, and since the bulk of the collection will tolerate at least −15°C, manual control is preferable. This means listening carefully to the local weather forecasts, which though not infallible have improved in recent years.

A refinement of the weather forecast is to install a maximum and minimum thermometer, for preference at bench height where the sun's rays will not distort the readings unduly. The white plastic models, whilst unattractive, are easier to read when anxiously checking the temperature late at night.

If very low overnight temperatures are likely and the fan heater is connected, then the thermostat means that the unit will cut in and out whenever the temperature is brought up to the minimum setting. The infrequency with which the operation of the heater is necessary makes cost – the usual criticism of the system – something of a side issue.

Some means of temperature control is, then, a useful refinement but by no means essential. Young or established plants, their root systems unable to support the top growth in severe weather, can be nurtured through spells that put paid to similar plants grown in alpine houses whose owners deem the use of any heat 'cheating'. Plants that produce new growth before our winters are half over – some growing thousands of metres higher in the mountains than their cultivated neighbours and that withstand virtually anything winter may bring – can receive the occasional protection without which severe damage would result. The history of alpine gardening is one littered with the corpses of countless introductions that fell victim to exceptional climatic conditions in their adoptive surroundings, and it is perhaps as well that we are now tentatively exploring a more flexible approach to the subject of cold hardiness.

4 Light and shade

One of the snags we run into when growing a diverse collection of alpines under one roof is how to satisfy their widely varying shade requirements. A whole range of opinions have been ventured, suggesting that summer scorch is caused by dryness at the root; that shading is really an admission that ventilation is inadequate, and that lowland sunshine is 'weaker' than the alpine version and as such should pose less of a problem. But trying to prescribe a practice that fits every alpine available is futile. They occupy different niches in the wild, have evolved adaptations to cope with intense sunlight and dryness, and will only grow satisfactorily in some instances if we recognise these differences.

To state the obvious: sun lovers often have a very small leaf area, the foliage may be reduced to needle-like spines or be covered in dense hairs with the margins inrolled, the lamina toughened and waxy. Plants used to more shaded conditions may have more thinly textured foliage that literally shrivels if exposed to strong sunlight (think of how the leaves of *Hepatica nobilis* die away as summer approaches unless kept in shade), and it matters not a jot whether the soil is moist or not. Woodlanders may have relatively large leaves, and in hot sunshine they droop: the roots simply cannot keep pace with the demand placed upon them and the margins and leaf tips may brown initially (*Cypripedium calceolus*, many gesneriads), this die back intensifying until cooler weather returns. The leaves may turn an unhealthy yellow-green, though if shading is provided they can revert within a matter of days, whereas these same conditions will not be appreciated by plants from the summit screes growing in pots nearby, which show a marked objection to any form of light restriction, sending out weak and straggly shoots that elongate dramatically, giving a horribly distorted version of the plant.

Even unshaded glass blocks some of the light. Depending on the angle of incidence when the sunlight reaches the glass, a maximum of 90 per cent transmission is possible, but the amount of ultra violet is much reduced. Not that all mountains are regularly bathed in sunlight, but when the mists and cloud do lift, the relatively clear light is less filtered, and the problem of heat being trapped – often the case in the greenhouse – does not occur.

One hears arguments that a shade plant from, say, central Afghanistan should be able to tolerate more sun in a cooler climate, but long experience suggests that many of the alpines we grow do need some protection from the high summer sun. They may be plants of the turf that survive best in a tangle of sheltering foliage, or of north- and east-facing vertical crevices (the opposite in the southern hemisphere) where the sun only shines for a few hours in the morning, they may be restricted to the forest margin or hang upside down in cave entrances.

The difficulty comes in balancing the danger of scorching against that of overdoing the shading, which not only causes a typically etiolated growth in some plants but can adversely affect the following season's flower production. Paradoxically, a really warm summer can, contrary to the popular theory, make matters worse if the grower over-compensates and blocks out too much light.

There are numerous means of providing shade for the alpine house, and their relevance is partially controlled by the amount of time the owner has available to spend at home to control their operation. To dispense briefly with those choices that I would not advocate:

(1) Any form of internal shading: this is likely to be unsuccessful (a scrim or light cloth on a ring pulley system is a commonly seen version) because it does not provide a barrier to prevent the sun from striking the glass, and in consequence the problem of temperature build-up is not solved.

(2) The paint-on preparations that are claimed to react to sunlight, clouding over when the sun shines and reverting to a near transparent phase when cloud cover increases: in my experience the claims made are over-optimistic.

(3) Wooden slatted blinds, worked by a sash cord system and kept clear of the upper lights by metal guide rails: these are difficult to find, costly to acquire and, over and above being treated with wood preservative, apt to require frequent maintenance to prevent jamming.

Much easier to handle is the fine green plastic netting specifically designed for the purpose, which can be bought by the roll and lasts well, although the odd tear is to be expected. Owners of wooden-structured alpine houses sometimes choose to pin lengths of this material to the outside, section by section, but it is much easier to find two pieces of dowelling the length of the house, measure the distance from the apex to the eave and down to the floor and affix the netting which will encompass this area (leaving some space for the windows to be opened) top and bottom. Four supporting brackets along the ridge hold the upper pole in place, and it is an easy matter for a person at either end to rewind the reel of material if a dull spell sets in. Shading is seldom necessary much before late spring, and is likely to be needed on and off until early autumn, when the sun can still be surprisingly strong. If the netting is stapled in a loop around the poles, it is relatively straightforward to pull it away and place it under cover for the winter. It is now possible to purchase custom-made widths of shading material, bound at the perimeter, with loopholes which attach to hooks along the greenhouse structure.

Because the netting lets in filtered light (it may be sold with an assessment of its light-admitting capacity such as '50 per cent shade') some gardeners prefer to risk leaving it on throughout the summer, siting plants that require higher light levels on the opposite benching. It is not necessary to shade the whole of the house; the southern and western aspects are of prime importance, with perhaps the roof area as a whole covered to fend off the meridian sun.

A less tidy solution, but one that continues to be adopted commercially and by a number of highly successful alpine house owners, is to use the white paint-on shading (sold in a powder under the tradename 'Coolglass' in Great Britain), which is diluted in water and can be applied at varying thicknesses. Advice to use it on the inside of the glass goes against the manufacturer's recommendations, and may be unnecessary since it is reasonably showerproof and can soon be reapplied, in the same way that five minutes with a housebrush will remove much of the covering in overcast periods. One has to question the plethora of advice against its use when faced with results that suggest it provides acceptable light levels for a wide range of alpines, which in the wild may in any case be found to seek some shelter if their ecology were to be studied in greater depth. Experience soon indicates those plants that are happier with higher light levels but are unlikely to enjoy the summer outdoors such as *Nototriche*, and these can be transferred to a well-ventilated frame if necessary.

It may be unavoidable that the alpine house receives shading from one aspect, perhaps because it has to be sited near to the dwelling or even as a lean-to, or, of it lies near to the boundary, because of trees in a neighbouring garden. Disregarding the autumn penance of leaves blowing in by the sackful, there may be some advantage in the light shade cast by deciduous trees, but the same cannot be said of evergreen foliage, and the rapid rise of an adjacent-growing conifer can be a particular nuisance. Where the light is one-directional, it is usual to turn the pots at regular intervals, to prevent lopsided growth, although it has a beneficial side effect in disturbing any roots that have started to anchor into the plunge. If there is no prospect of improving the incident light, it would be as well to confine your choice to alpines that will grow well in at least light shade, which is far more sensible than struggling against the odds to produce sun-loving plants in reasonable fettle.

5 Watering

The amount of water a plant receives, and when that watering is administered, is frequently singled out as the most important aspect of cultivation. There is something in this, but it should be seen as an interrelated discipline, depending on the local conditions under which you garden, the size and age of the plant, the potting compost, the season and numerous other factors. One can give broad rules, and advise on how to judge when a plant needs water, but specific recommendations along the lines of 'water twice a week' are nonsensical. The degree of precision needed has been somewhat overemphasised: the sheer frequency of the operation means that mistakes will be made, but it is usually the long-term strategy that counts rather than an occasional hiccup in the system. Letting a plant in full growth dry out completely is the exception – in strong sunlight combined with high temperatures a plant can be killed outright within the space of a day. The frequently heard advice to apply water frugally after mid-summer is baffling and takes little account of the high temperatures of an 'Indian' summer, or the secondary spurt of growth seen in many plants surprisingly late in the season.

The first thing to note is that whilst each plant is best judged individually when assessing its watering needs, even a small collection can number several hundred pots, and if just half that number have to be picked up, scrutinised and possibly placed in a soak tray, then the procedure will be impossibly time consuming. In practice, if the compost is well drained, and assuming the plant is not at rest, it should be possible to water without too much pause for pondering. Exceptions to the rule – those plants that for much of the year dislike water lodging in their foliage, for instance, or those that seem to prefer the compost to give up much of its moisture content before the next deluge – can, with experience, be identified and singled out for more cautious treatment.

Looking for advice when I first grew alpines under glass, I found that there were two recognised methods of judging when to water, neither of which I have ever seen fit to adopt. The first relies on the weight of the pot, with a heavy pot in theory indicating the soil was amply moist – this might be easy to judge with a small pot, but is progressively less helpful as the larger pots, which are heavy enough empty, are reached. Since the composts used are not standardised, some degree of variation can be expected, and by the time one has allowed for the topdressing and in some cases the sheer bulk of the plant, the method becomes impossible. The second method envisages tapping lightly on the side of the pot and listening for either a light ringing sound or a dull thud, the former indicating that the plant needs watering. Presumably this is rather like perfect pitch – you are either born with it, in which case there is clear division of right and wrong, or you are not, and must make do with other means of judging the issue. The important distinctions to be made are between hand watering and automated watering, and the amount given during late spring, summer and early autumn contrasted with that applied in the winter.

Anyone who has spent some time in mountainous regions will know that in addition to water percolating through the soil from snowmelt, very heavy thunderstorms, caused when saturated air sheds its load as it rises (orographic rainfall), are a feature of some areas. This has the reverse effect in the rainshadow on the other side of the higher mountains (and some regions experience a parching summer), but in general the plants when in flower are used to a steady supply of moisture. However, plants are very seldom found where water collects and stagnates. Even where the ground appears permanently saturated, the water is invariably moving; draining away down the slopes to be replaced by highly oxygenated supplies from above. Where precipitation levels are lower, the moisture-holding capacity of what at first sight may appear to be arid scree is often surprisingly high, and heavy mists often have a significant effect when trapped by the densely hairy leaf surfaces that characterise the plants of such regions.

All this means that it helps considerably to find out where the plants grow in the wild, and how they behave in their natural surroundings. Reproducing the exact conditions is clearly out of the question, but we can simulate the more important details with fair success. For instance, a high proportion of alpines with swollen tap-roots favour well-drained sites. If the soil becomes so wet that the oxygen content of the medium drops, metals and toxins can sometimes form which on occasion rupture the cell walls, allowing the accumulated sugars to leak to the area around the root where they attract fungal diseases. Other plants need a cool, moist microclimate – many of the Petiolarid primulas are unable to regulate their metabolic rate and when the temperature rises, the roots cannot always keep pace with the demand for water. Under such conditions spraying the foliage with fine cooling mist and shading the plants is preferable to heavy-handed watering.

The compromise usually arrived at is to make the compost freer-draining than is strictly necessary. This helps to counteract over-watering with sensitive species, but means that the collection has to be regularly monitored for signs of dryness.

In the summer, the situation can be eased by moving as many plants as possible into uncovered plunge beds. Here they can safely be watered with a garden sprinkler system during hot weather. What can be grown outside during this season varies from area to area, but always think twice before subjecting to this treatment any plant with:

(1) A summer dormancy – not just those plants that aestivate completely but

including the many that shrivel back to drought-resistant buds or simply shut down when the temperature rises, waiting for cooler weather before visible signs of growth recommence.

(2) Leaves that are in any way felted or densely hairy, this often indicating an adaptation to the intense insolation of their homeland, which leads on to

(3) A habitat that takes in the desert fringes, summer dry upland areas or mountains where high temperatures coupled with strong winds soon remove surface water brought by the occasional storms.

(4) A preference for growing on vertical cliff faces (chasmophytes) or the entrance overhang of caves; in such cases it is unusual for the foliage to remain sodden for days on end as it sometimes can in lowland gardens.

One could argue that dionysias from the southern reaches of Iran and nototriches from outlying areas of the Atacama have occasionally been persuaded to accept outdoor cultivation, but on the whole such experiments have ended in failure, and with species only tenuously in cultivation it makes little sense unless results under glass are unpromising.

With such plants, it is usual to avoid overhead watering, since moisture lodging in the leaf bases and around the crown can induce rotting at almost any time of the year. The general method is to trickle water around the edge of the pot with a small, long-spouted watering can, allowing it to seep down progressively rather than flooding the surface. Greater control can be exercised by partially blocking the spout with the tip of the index finger, allowing a fine jet of water to emit. If the compost surface slopes away from the neck of the plant, then the dyke created around the perimeter will allow the water to drain away without coming into contact with the caudex. Some growers purposely excavate a small peripheral trough and fill this with water, allowing the contents to drain completely and refilling several times, which is worthwhile with the comparatively few plants that react badly to the presence of surface moisture at almost any time of the year.

In general, water is given when the compost at the edge of the pots is barely damp to the touch – by winter, when evaporation is often low and the plants' need for water reduced, this degree of moisture will be ideal for the majority, but for the period February to late October in the northern hemisphere (and especially in the run up to flowering time) any dryness at the root can prove fatal. By no means all alpines have evolved the massive root systems that enable them to obtain moisture at depth, and pot-grown plants are always vulnerable to drought.

A moisture-rententive plunge material provides a way of allowing plants grown in pots with absorbent walls to take in extra water, but the advice to water only the plunge should be treated with caution. Plants in large pots, for example, are seldom plunged more than half way, and the amount of water that permeates through the pot wall is seldom adequate for their needs. Here the answer is often to lift the pot off the bench and stand it in a soak tray (a washing-up bowl will do) so that the water comes at least half way up the side of the pot. With those species that form roots adventitiously above the soil surface from the nodes, it is worth completely submerging the plant for a minute or so, which is perfectly safe in the growing season, and has the advantage of allowing dead leaves and the odd slug or other pest to come floating to the surface. Indeed, for those plants that only really need alpine house protection to shelter their blooms from harsh weather or a summer downpour, wetting the foliage is a useful means of locally counteracting the drying atmosphere that other inhabitants need to thrive. Just about any plant with a glossy leaf surface, or whose leaves expand considerably after flowering, is liable to need this treatment. Moreover, there are several plant families of which virtually every member has this requirement – Diapensiaceae, Ericaceae and Gentianaceae being of greatest significance where the alpine gardener is concerned.

One other point: the use of water straight from the tap is often criticised, both because the supplies are nowadays on the whole chlorinated and, in some areas, charged with lime that manifests itself in the furring on the inside of kettles. Many people in hard-water areas experience little sign of chlorosis in their plants, perhaps giving an application of sequestered iron once or twice in the season with plants known to grow on acid soils. Other prefer to connect the downpipe from the guttering of the alpine house to a water butt (standard models have a capacity of 182 litres), turning to the main water supply only when this source has been exhausted.

'Automatic' watering

Often this term is used loosely to mean anything other than watering by hand, but truly automated watering systems involve the dual use of a mains water supply and an electrical control. Water floods through a valve that opens and shuts in response to a pre-set timer (often unsatisfactory), using paired float switches on the header tank or, probably best of all in that account is taken of the plunge material's degree of saturation, two electrodes that govern the opening of the solenoid valve, with the upper shutting off the supply when the water table reaches its level, and the lower activating the flow when it drops below. For this it is essential that the bench is level.

Put briefly, the bench is lined with heavy-duty plastic, and the pots plunged in sand – other materials such as expanded clay granules and grit are occasionally used. Note that capillary matting is seldom satisfactory: moisture barely rises high enough in the larger sizes of plant pot, even if a glassfibre wick is inserted through the drainage hole, and in very warm weather the system does not always keep pace with water displacement. A syphon tank is connected up to the mains water supply (cheaper versions required manual refilling of their reservoirs), and from this leads either (1) a length of tubing that extends down the centre of the benching, perforated, or (very rarely) porous, which is buried in the plunge. (2) a point watering system, less popular and generally speaking a temporary measure to tide over the gardener's short-term absence. The tubing, which must *never* be translucent since algae growth will soon cause blockages, lies on the surface, with a series of small tributary 'feeders' with adjustable nozzles, sometimes placed directly onto the soil surface of the pot, but often used to keep the surrounding plunge moist.

Whichever is chosen the normal practice is to disconnect during the winter months. There is a reluctance to use these systems because they 'average out' rather than gauging the needs of the individual plant, although approximate control can be achieved with a capillary bench by varying the depth of the plunge, and with point watering by varying the rate of flow through the 20 or more nozzles that a typical system involves. None the less, they bring a measure of reliability for those who cannot provide their plants with attention on an almost daily basis, and are useful to those gardeners who enjoy lengthy holidays when a combination of heatwaves and inexperienced/inattentive plantminders might otherwise cause havoc.

6 Food and Nutrition

There is frequently a pronounced relationship between plant and soil type, to the extent that some species act as indicators of a specific stratum or topsoil structure – being found nowhere else, even when conditions for growth seem outwardly ideal.

Whatever the mitigating influence of variables such as competition from other plants, climate and aspect, there is ample evidence to confirm the choosiness of numerous alpines. We read of plants that exist only on gypsum deposits, salt flats, sandstone cliffs, limestome screes, in peaty turf, pine needle duff, adobe clay and almost any other rock or soil type one might care to list. Just a few metres away from where one species is thriving, the different soil conditions can inspire the development of a quite distinct plant community, and this pronounced bond might be expected to cause trouble when the same plants are attempted in cultivation.

Rather surprisingly, the vast majority of alpines will consent to grow reasonably in a standardised potting compost, notwithstanding a high degree of specialisation in their natural choice of soil type. There has been a gradual movement away from the complicated array of ingredients (often difficult to obtain) once thought necessary, and there is now a broad consensus of agreement on the shortlist of more important materials from which the gardener can choose. Locally available alternatives may have to be used, notably in the type of stone chippings that can be obtained, for it is clearly impractical to import from a distance, when the cost of transportation can outweigh the actual value of the materials.

Compost

The first essential is that the compost constituents should be easily and reliably available in the immediate area. This rules out a number of the ingredients that have been advanced as indispensable in the past – Cornish silver sand and pumice among them. The properties of aeration and drainage which their use implies can be duplicated by other materials.

Most gardeners settle down to using one or two basic compost formulae, often varying the proportions to deal with the perceived needs of certain plants. This usually means altering the proportion of grit or sand to be included. To function properly, the roots require air and a well-drained compost where the moisture does not compact and which maintains an open pore structure. When the compost is drained to 'container capacity' – i.e. when all free water has drained away – it has been estimated that the amount of air contained in the pore spaces should not fall between 10–15 per cent of the whole. Coarse ingredients – principally grit of 3mm or above – have a dual function, enabling water to drain away and opening up the pore structure. The humus content can act similarly and it is striking how seldom alpines are found in waterlogged soils. There are a few notable exceptions: in the European Alps, one can come across wide stands of *Ranunculus glacialis* and *Soldanella alpina* flowering whilst partially submerged, but even here this is usually a short-lived feature associated with snowmelt. More commonly, the water will be highly oxygenated and constantly percolating through the root zone.

It is possible to determine the air-filled porosity of the compost by weighing a pot full of saturated soil, then reweighing it a few hours later when container capacity has been reached, and the third time emptying out the compost, inserting a polythene bag liner and adding water to the level of the old compost before reweighing. The empty pot weight is checked, deducted from each of the three figures, and the percentage value obtained by noting the discrepancy between the first two figures, multiplying by 100, and using this as the top half of a fraction, where the bottom is the weight of the water-filled pot.

In practice few gardeners bother with such experiments; since we know little about the optimum structure for any given plant, common sense based on experience has to serve. For the majority of plants, a compost comprising 50 per cent chippings of 3mm grist or above has been found satisfactory. This is the basis for many of the composts recommended down the years, a fact sometimes obscured by the materials recommended, often in precise quantities, for the remaining half.

The pea gravel sometimes used for surfacing driveways may be all that is available and although it is a variable material, often containing sandstone and limestone, it can be used with reasonable results. For preference, however, a 'sharp' neutral grit that does not affect the pH of the compost is chosen, and here the choice is generally between granite in various grades and crushed quartzite, which is usually sold as potting grit.

Such materials may seem difficult to obtain but the likelihood is that if the local garden centre or nursery cannot supply them, then a builders' merchant may be able to do so. Other people recommend pet shops, which frequently stock a suitable product under the name 'turkey grit'. The only reservation is that quantities provided are usually meagre, making this a very costly choice.

Anyone who owns a trailer or can cope with the large quantities involved will buy their grit loose by the ton, but it may be worth paying out the extra money and obtaining it ready bagged, which helps greatly with handling and makes storage a tidier business. Several grades of these chippings are usually offered, and when ordering it is wise to check whether the material is washed or not. In some instances – unwashed granite chippings for example – the finer material provides a medium reminiscent of the graded material of a terminal moraine, but crushed quartzite in particular may be mixed with a sandy clay that is unsightly as a topdressing and clogging if added to the compost.

Most of the above are lime-free – something one should check before purchasing from an unfamiliar source. It is as well to be wary before adding limestone chippings to the compost of almost any plant, even if it is said to be calcifuge in its natural habitats. Limestones, after all, vary considerably: some are more soluble than others, and this may partly explain why some Himalayan rhododendrons grow happily among limestone rocks in the wild, but can show signs of chlorosis if a similar arrangement is attempted in the garden. The amount of free lime in the soil can also influence the intensity of the flower colour, something familiar to those who grow *Meconopsis*. With plants from the high alpine screes and rock crevices, the proportion of grit is frequently increased to 75 per cent. Conversely, for those few species that inhabit bogs but still make good alpine house plants, like *Anagallis tenella*, the chippings content is greatly reduced.

Attempts to provide efficient drainage without creating a compost that dries out completely have led to experiments that incorporate a number of mineral aggregates. They also serve to improve aeration and, being slightly acidic, are compatible with a wide range of alpines. Perlite is probably the best known, along with vermiculite, but heat-treated arcillite and montmorillonite are becoming increasingly important. Their traditional usage has been in improving the aeration of peat-based composts, but for plants which inhabit soils with a high mineral content they have been used as a substitute for the peat, forming perhaps 25 per cent of the bulk of the compost. Being so light, there is an appreciable weight advantage against more established materials, most keenly felt when attempting to lift the larger pots. Nor do they compact, unlike composts usually composed of peat, where the initial 'openness' is soon lost. The light and open structure they provide frequently results in substantial root development. Although these aggregates do not break down in the soil, doubts remain about their long-term use – it has been queried, for example, whether or not toxic substances are gradually absorbed and retained by the particles.

The use of aggregates seems to be on the increase, to the extent that perlite is sometimes incorporated as a constituent of John Innes potting compost, which flies in the face of the strictly formulated set of ingredients. Indeed, if your intention is to use this product as a base, then be aware that the quality is not always as consistent as one might expect, and those that sprout a fine crop of bittercress when moistened (inadequately sterilised) or 'pan' when dry (too much clay in the loam) are by no means unknown. Each bag should be checked before use and if its contents smell sour, or form a resilient plug when slightly moistened and a small quantity lightly compacted in the palm of the hand, reject them.

For all this, there is widespread support for John Innes potting composts Nos 1, 2 and 3 (with the latter often favoured for slow-growing plants that are repotted infrequently) used in combination with other ingredients. Warnings that they are carefully balanced and should not be modified can be discounted.

It is generally easier to use them as 'loam' when making up a compost, rather than going to the trouble of stacking turves, waiting for the grass to rot down, and then sterilising the soil as it is required. The local topsoil may not be suitable, either in texture or pH value, whereas John Innes (in theory, anyway) does provide some uniformity; and although the formulation includes a small amount of ground chalk, by the time the other materials have been added, it does not usually prove harmful, even to lime-hating plants.

Loam-based composts are still favoured by an overwhelming majority of alpine gardeners. They are not, however, used universally. Several groups of plants that naturally inhabit soils with a high humus content tend to prefer a similar rooting medium in cultivation. For plants that grow in woodland areas, the majority of those that are found in areas of high rainfall, and genera that predominantly grow in soils with a low proportion of loam (*Androsace*, for example) it is standard practice to use some form of organic matter for the body of the compost.

Some gardeners have gone further and use a loam-free compost across the board, irrespective of whether the plant they are attempting to grow is found naturally in heavy clay, river shingle or whatever. Quite apart from the short-term composts sold for raising annuals and houseplants, several other products can be adapted for this use. They may be labelled 'Ericaceous compost' or similar, and their friable structure and ability to hold water is of more consequence than the added nutrients and trace elements. Although there is an element of sharp sand included, grit has to be added to supplement the drainage at anything up to three parts per one of compost when growing high alpines. The exact proportions are not critical, except to say that the ingredients are measured out by bulk and not weight. Not all plants will appreciate the low nutrient levels that result, and the restrained use of a liquid fertiliser may be necessary.

The organic material usually recommended is leafmould, but there are disadvantages associated with its use, and it is by no means essential. The layer of decomposed leaves that collects in a deciduous woodland is most commonly meant, and oak or beech are favoured, but these may not be available and other materials such as composted pine needles can be substituted.

Whatever the source, the leafmould generally has to be put through a garden sieve to remove stones and snapped off twigs. It is also likely to be home for a number of pests, fungi which can damage plants, and dormant seeds. To dispense with these, it is necessary partially to sterilise the soil. Chemicals such as formalin can be obtained to assist this process, but they are not very pleasant to handle, and very few amateurs utilise them. Conversely, heat sterilisation is set to gain in popularity now that the microwave oven has come into our lives, and can remove primary pests without overcooking the soil.

The leafmould is placed in a suitable microwave container and left in the oven until the temperature of the interior reaches approx. 82°C. A temperature of just 55°C will see off any earthworms or insect pests, but this will not for instance kill weed seeds. If a conventional oven is used it is hard to control the temperature properly, and instead the usual advice is to construct a two-tier container on the same principle as a fish steamer, with the lower half filled with water, brought to the boil over a heat source. The upper half has a perforated base which allows the steam to invade the material, and again use of the thermometer prevents the temperature from going beyond the minimum necessary to kill off the worst of the pathogens.

There are both physical and chemical consequences of heat sterilisation. These are by turns beneficial (increased ability to absorb moisture, higher levels of phosphorous and potassium made available) and potentially harmful (initial increase in the level of ammonium compounds, especially if the material is too moist when sterilised). The effect of the treatment is cumulative and once the desired temperature has been reached, the treated material should be left to cool in the open, best achieved by spreading it thinly on heavy-duty polythene sacking. Some degree of reinfection is to be expected, but if stored in bags this will not present undue problems and, contrary to some reports, keeping qualities are good provided the material is kept under cover.

Why anyone goes to all this trouble when a bag of peat and a slow-release fertiliser work equally well is mystifying. I am convinced that, treated sensibly, a plant grown in the latter performs every bit as ably. And because the product is clearly defined and consistent, setbacks such as a poor batch or one with an unexpectedly high pH (the classic failing with leafmould which continues to catch gardeners out) are unlikely. Moreover, pending recent concern over its continued large scale harvesting, it is widely available and not unduly expensive, at least not in the relatively small quantities required in the alpine house. A couple of the 200-litre 'maxibales' should see the average gardener comfortably through the year.

Some people use the various sedge peats successfully, but the general preference is for sphagnum moss peats, which provide little in the way of plant food but, if care is taken not to overcompress, produce a friable compost that holds water well without becoming waterlogged. This is not to deny that drying out can present difficulties, and it is generally true that soilless composts require most exact handling in this respect. The balance of grit and coarse silver sand helps to keep the compost open and aids the general absorption of water, which can be otherwise awkward if it is allowed to dry out.

The minimal levels of nutrition provided are not always as disadvantageous as might be imagined – plants like *Briggsia muscicola* have been grown in pure sphagnum for a couple of years without any supplementary feeding, and have still developed to flowering size. Shortage of nitrogen can occur, and to counteract this a pinch of hoof and horn is often added. Plants that thrive on a richer diet (often those that naturally inhabit the upper pastures) can sometimes benefit from the addition of well-rotted cow manure, now available quite widely in a dried and composted state. The safest rule is first to appreciate the plants' natural soil type, for a few alpines would react adversely to such an additive, either losing their normal appearance or failing outright.

Because peat is somewhat acidic (unlike certain of the commercial *peat-*

based composts, where calcium carbonate is added), the hoof and horn is sometimes replaced with bonemeal, which again is slow acting and unlikely to be over administered. It is also possible to obtain fritted trace elements which have been fused into minute particles of glass. These are routinely added to soilless composts (at the rate of 1.4g per litre), just as slow release fertilisers, based on varying ratios of nitrogen, phosphates and potassium (NPK) are usually included for the general run of alpines. A formula low in nitrogen is recommended, and anything in the region of 12.5:25:25 is likely to prove suitable.

Supplementary feeding

This leads on to the subject of supplementary feeding, a vexed one because the results of incautious application are all too familiar. It is easy to overdo the quantities, which seldom leads to a better plant. You either use a liquid fertiliser in response to a signal from the plant that it is undernourished, principally indicated by unhealthy or poorly developed foliage, steady loss of vigour and a fall-off in the amount of flowers produced. Or you map out a programme from the outset, recognising that some plants quickly exhaust the nutrients in their compost, and others have specific needs at certain stages in this development – bulbs after flowering is completed, for instance.

All manner of complicated routines are worked out, some using one fertiliser up to bud set, another until the flowers develop and a third thereafter. Much room for experimentation still exists, always remembering that smaller and slower-growing plants in particular will seldom respond favourably to these antics. It would be as well to conduct a trial by applying any unfamiliar compound at half the manufacturer's recommended dosage on a couple of spare plants, and allowing up to a month before deciding whether to extend the treatment.

The fertilisers available have increased dramatically in recent years, and the period of adjusting to their use has thrown up some unedifying sights – lewisias with spindly stems, once-dwarf Narcissus whose flowers are hidden among a shock of over-developed leaves, and supposedly compact plants like the various species of *Townsendia* sporting lush foliage and flowering stems several times their proper height.

Of those foliar feeds that serve to correct a deficiency, chelated iron (normally combined with manganese and magnesium) is a well-established means of remedying chlorosis, caused by an inappropriately alkaline soil or (rarely) faulty root action. One or two doses during the growing season are enough to solve the chlorophyll deficiency, and precise dosages are unnecessary. It is now possible to purchase a liquid seaweed extract that includes an iron deficiency corrective.

Equally familiar are the liquid manure preparations more often connected with the cultivation of houseplants, which generally err too much in favour of the nitrogen part of the formulation, but seem to suit many of the woodland

and 'hungrier' plants. Numerous species of *Primula* have relished this diet when either rootbound or coping with the effects of old age, and cultivars of *P. marginata* such as 'Pritchards Variety' seem to appreciate this supplementary nutrition providing that it takes place after flowering. This holds true of many gesneriads (*Ramonda*, × *Briggandra*, *Sarmienta*) and plants of the rich upland pasture such as *Soldanella alpina*.

Latterly the various brands of tomato fertiliser, high in potash, have come to the fore, and whilst their usage is optional, for many bulbous plants there is a definite advantage in regular dosages after flowering until dormancy. Good results have been obtained by watering a wide range of alpines with the same substances, perhaps two or three times in the early summer, at intervals of at least a fortnight, but many very successful cultivators would say that such treatment is unnecessary. On the other hand, watering with a solution of sulphate of potash in the weeks preceding dormancy is said to improve flowering, and there is evidence to suggest that it is a worthwhile activity.

This list by no means exhausts the possible materials used in making up composts for alpines and concoctions to supplement their feeding. It is difficult to think of many plants that need an 'individual' compost differing fundamentally from that used for the other occupants of the alpine house, and many will thrive in a standard mix without any modification. Nevertheless, few gardeners can resist moving beyond precise formulae and judging by sight and touch to make sure the mix is satisfactory. Until experience is gained, enabling sufficient confidence to determine what is and what is not satisfactory, the recipes contained in virtually every book on alpine plants can be useful if the materials are procurable.

7 Pests and Diseases

Those gardeners who imagine that the alpine house provides living quarters solely for their plants soon learn otherwise. A considerable range of small invertebrates – by no means all harmful to alpines but customarily labelled pests if they wriggle, jump, fly or crawl – find shelter and a ready food source in even the most regulated glasshouse, and their eradication (or at least control) presupposes a vigilant attitude throughout the year.

We are often consoled by the advice that healthy plants are resistant to attack – an over-optimistic viewpoint not always borne out by the evidence. Although it is certainly true that much can be done to keep infection and infestations at bay, I doubt if any seasoned gardener has managed to avoid serious damage to his or her plants at some stage. Much the same could be said of the relatively few diseases to which alpine plants are prone. What distinguishes those collections which rally and prosper is their owners' ability to diagnose the problem at an earlier stage and take the appropriate course of action.

Specialist gardeners often bemoan the resilience of the pests and diseases that thrive in the monoculture provided for them. In the alpine house, by contrast, a wide variety of genera are normally gathered together, and this diversity helps to check the spread of any given menace. In passing, it is worth noting that a widespread disorder may well be the result of physiological ills rather than the consequence of some mystifying pest. Keeping the alpine house insufficiently shaded, subjecting the occupants to water stress, administering an unsuitable fertiliser; these and a host of other oversights can produce symptoms that are not always easy to trace to their real source.

Rather than listing the wide array of ailments that once in a while afflict alpine plants, it seems more sensible to indicate the principal pests and diseases that most gardeners are likely to encounter. Their populations rise and fall in line with the prevailing weather pattern, but of course the alpine gardener is not simply at the mercy of the climate, for much can be done to modify the microclimate of the alpine house.

Pests

Most pests are much more difficult to spot than the symptoms of their presence: the distorted or dismembered leaf is readily apparent, but the organism that caused the damage sometimes proves more elusive. In the majority of cases, the method of feeding provides a broad clue – between those which suck out the sap and those which chew away wholeheartedly for instance – and some predators have a highly distinctive trademark that immediately incriminates them. The silvery trail of a slug, the gummed foliage surrounding a caterpillar pupa, or the notched leaves left by the adult vine weevil – such signs eliminate all other suspects.

What is sometimes forgotten is the complication of a secondary malady resulting from the initial attack. Virus particles are occasionally transmitted via the aphid stylet; leafhoppers have been implicated in the spread of what in laymen's terms appear to be virus-related organisms known as mycoplasmas; and botrytis habitually infects the snags of pest-damaged foliage.

A visit to any alpine habitat soon dispels the myth that such places are pest free, but it is nevertheless true that under lowland conditions plants from these regions are subject to an unfamiliar range of predators. Any native population develops an inbuilt resistance to certain ailments (think of the innoculations travellers are advised to have before leaving home) and it should not surprise that first-generation introductions of some plants have difficulty in adapting.

Probably the most tenacious threat comes from the numerous species of **aphid**, winged and wingless, that under glass ignore the rules about being active only in spring and summer. Even so, their ability to reproduce increases dramatically during warm weather. Usually it is the new growth that first becomes infested, although the underside of almost any leaf seems vulnerable, causing the familiar puckering and discolouration as sap is siphoned away. References to root aphids are somewhat misleading in that several species are involved, not all of them confined to the root zone throughout their life cycle. Some genera – and especially those belonging to the *Primulaceae* – play host to these pests, their presence sometimes advertised around the crown by accretions of grey or near-opaque aphids surrounded by a nimbus of powdery white deposits. Uncovering the root system will reveal colonies spread discontinuously along the entire length. Pot-grown plants have a marked incidence of these clusters where the roots touch and grow parallel to the inner wall.

Next in importance are the several red spider mites, most notably the **glasshouse red spider mite**: in the British Isles these pests are not indigenous, but have prospered since their arrival and are now an increasing problem even on outdoor crops. The suggestion that the hibernating mites are severely affected by average winter temperatures, or that moist conditions alone will halt their spread, are now outdated. Little more than half a millimetre long at maturity, they are difficult to discern with the naked eye. The first indication is usually a loss of lustre from the leaf surface, progressing through mottled discoloration (as if a light dusting of flour had been applied) until the lifeless leaf withers away. It is usually those alpines with a relatively thin leaf blade that are worst affected: *Townsendia*, *Viola*, *Lupinus*, *Draba* and *Dianthus* are often the first to be affected, and other genera – *Daphne*, for example – may be defoliated in a way one seldom sees in open ground specimens. Colonies pepper the undersides of the leaves in the early stages, and the fine webbing they produce can coat much of the plant if left unchecked. Temperatures of

30°C are regularly reached in the alpine house in the vast majority of summers and under these conditions a red spider mite egg develops into a functioning adult in little more than a week.

Another pest in the ascendant is the **vine weevil**, sometimes seen as the centimetre-long, brownish-black adult that feigns death if uncovered, but more often detected, belatedly, as one of up to a dozen off-white, c-shaped grubs feeding on the last remnants of the fleshy root system just below the surface of the soil. The larvae are most active outside the summer months, and mature over a period of several months, favouring the slightly moist, humus-rich composts that are used in the cultivation of their favourite diet of *Cyclamen*, *Primula*, *Shortia* and the like. Sometimes the rootless remains provide suitable propagating material even in the depths of winter: this is certainly true of *Soldanella*, which if placed in a mixture of peat and sand will send down fresh roots and grow away happily in the springtime. Soil from the infected site should be discarded, for whilst the larvae may all have been found and despatched, further eggs may still remain in the compost, and these are all but invisible except when first laid.

Snails and more commonly **slugs** inflict the most severe and immediate damage, completely removing the topgrowth of even established plants between supper and breakfast time. The problem is lessened in alpine houses where the plants rest on staging, although if the benches rest on brick pillars slugs can assuredly manage the vertical ascent. More commonly, pots transferred from another area of the garden harbour either adults or the transparent eggs, sometimes nestled in the drainage hole but frequently more cunningly concealed. Most of the species feed both above and below ground. It is rare to experience a persistent problem from this source in the glasshouse. Small garden slugs sometimes escape detection and have a predilection for grazing on the flowerbuds of a whole host of alpines, and shade-loving genera like *Ramonda* that are on occasion kept below the staging need more than usual care if they are not to fall victim. But in general the alpine house can serve as a refuge for those plants (many species of *Campanula*, for example) that cannot be satisfactorily grown in the open garden for this very reason.

Sporadic attacks by **caterpillars** can be expected throughout the year. Several names crop up repeatedly, in particular the larvae of the large yellow underwing moth which improve on the efforts of vine weevil grubs by not only feeding on corms and rootstocks, earning them the name cutworms, but extend their efforts to include the foliage as well. Measuring some 5cm, they are perhaps the largest caterpillars to pay an unwelcome visit to the alpine house, and their appetite is voracious. The much smaller larvae of the carnation tortrix moth are also troublesome, and apart from *Dianthus* can be expected to appear on *Daphne*, *Primula* and various members of the *Leguminosae*. Because the moths are inconspicuous and nocturnal, the first sign of trouble is often the gummed foliage in which the caterpillar endeavours to pupate after feeding in the leaf axils. The principal danger period is from mid summer on into the autumn, but in a mild winter these limits are not observed.

Birds prove troublesome in some areas, principally in the spring, when the woolly rosettes of certain cushion plants provide useful nesting material, and many gardeners stretch some netting over the doorway – a precaution that has never proved necessary in my garden. **Earwigs** tend to blemish plants rather than threaten their general well-being, sap-sucking **thrips** have a similar nuisance value, and peat-based composts have proved congenial for the larvae of the **sciarid fly**. Owners of miniature rock gardens under glass find from time to time that **ants' nests** become established, and any plant in the vicinity is liable to suffer, though whether from localised drought caused by the ants tunnelling activities or (as one theory advances) a build-up of formic acid remains a moot point. Bulb enthusiasts dread the ominous hum of the **narcissus fly**, and the autumn active **carnation fly** has grubs that make mischief with their burrowing activities – as much a hazard for the genus *Lewisia* as their nominate host, but the only other widespread pest is the **stem eelworm**.

Those eelworms parasitic on plants feed both externally and, in the case of the above, internally on plant tissues, and manifest their presence in the general ill-health of the specimen infected. With *Saxifraga*, the genus most likely to be affected in the alpine house, parts of the cushion often turn yellow and die away, flowering is impaired and those blooms that develop are typically distorted, in some instances the pedicel failing to extend to its customary length. The many bulbs affected have distorted foliage that dies down early, often commencing as the flowers are produced, and checking beneath the soil surface reveals a rather flaccid bulb – the consequence of dead tissue that may spread until the bulb perishes since the eelworm, or nematode, is able to survive for several years in the form of a cyst. Great care must be taken to prevent cross contamination, for although the adults can move over short distances, spread is principally by mechanical transfer. A wide range of alpines is susceptible, but some rather puzzling exceptions are known. With the Porophyllum saxifrages, for example, *S. burseriana* cultivars are seldom affected. Breeding resistant clones is a well-tried procedure in other branches of horticulture, and there is scope for greater experiment with alpine plants. A distressing side-effect of stem eelworm infestation lies in their ability to transmit several harmful viruses.

Viruses

In recent years there has been increasing talk of virus-affected stocks, notably with garden cultivars of the genus *Primula*, and it is likely that these submicroscopic organisms have infiltrated a variety of alpine plants. There are several means of transmitting a virus to other plants, but the most frequent is via invertebrate activity, the agent in question being termed the vector. Alpine gardeners are likely to see the effects of **tomato mosaic virus** and **cucumber mosaic virus** – the names deriving from the first hosts on which they were found and classified.

Aphids are the principal vectors, heading a list which goes on to include

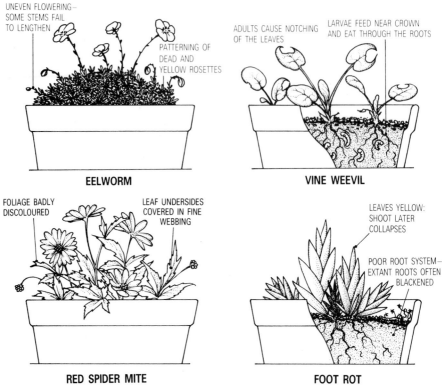

Figure 5   Plant ailments

leaf hoppers, certain mites and thrips. Systemic insecticides are frequently recommended to check the spread of viruses via these sources, which always seems rather a peculiar defence: by the time the insects' mandibles have made contact with leaf, the damage is done . . . even if revenge follows shortly afterwards.

It is rare for a virus to kill the plant affected, but in some instances the disruption to the general appearance of infected specimens renders them worthless. Viruses are said to be latent when they are present in plant tissue without causing obvious defects beyond a slowing down of growth and, usually, the host's impaired ability to produce flowers. Active virus infection manifests itself in a variety of ways, among which the most familar are shortening of the petals; discolouration, streaking and colour breaking of the corolla; leaf crinkling; uneven distribution of chlorophyll (seen as mottling, striping or banding along the veins); and buckling or contortion of the stems.

Vegetative propagation normally passes on these defects, which is why old cultivars are frequently said to be less attractive or vigorous than they were in their heyday, and although raising stock from seed often removes all trace of virus, some of the more significant strains (tomato mosaic virus included) can be passed on in this manner. Fortunately, virus particles are unevenly distributed in a plant's system, and since in many cases they do not invade the growing tip (or meristem), this can be removed and increased greatly by micropropagation to provide 'clean' stocks. Such techniques are already operated by a number of amateur gardeners, and as the principles become more widely understood, one would expect use of this method to spread.

Diseases

The tendency is for gardening books to advise somewhat frostily that pests and diseases only visit themselves on the negligent gardener. Concerning pests this attitude is hard to understand, but it has to be said that with diseases it is frequently what we neglect to do that leads to their establishment. The spores are carried in the air throughout the year but they are opportunist and will germinate only under certain conditions. Leaving snags of dead foliage on a plant, overwatering on clammy, windless days and failing to provide adequate ventilation all create the conditions under which fungal diseases thrive. And once they are established, their removal is a difficult and time-consuming chore.

Of all the fungal diseases, **botrytis** affects occupants of the alpine house more than any other. Because it thrives under conditions of high relative humidity coupled with an abundance of dead foliage, it is frequently regarded as a problem confined to the winter months. This is not altogether true: the spores will germinate at temperatures of up to 25°C, and are merely reliant on a damp, generally still atmosphere. One sees its development, for example, on some *Campanula* species, where the solid covering of spent flowerheads can, if left, quickly become infected. Lower temperatures associated with the winter months are only significant in that (a) frost damage commonly provides an entry point for the spores and (b) humidity tends to be higher in the coldest parts of the alpine house. The common name – Grey Mould Rot – is as concise a description of the consequences of its establishment as could be attempted. In crowded conditions, such as a fully tenanted glasshouse, it can spread rapidly. Spores have the ability to germinate within two hours of settling, living saprophytically on dead foliage before invading living tissue unless checked. Bulbs sometimes succumb when the leaf bases are affected, and even if they survive defoliation, small black *sclerotia* able to survive the summer dormancy can sometimes be found clinging to their outer walls, ready to cause trouble during the next growing season.

Powdery mildew can be equally pervasive, the spores needing no more than an intermittent breeze to launch themselves onto surrounding hosts. Again, high humidity is a precondition for its spread, but unlike botrytis the spores germinate best on dry surfaces – indeed the infective spores can be washed off, which partially explains why mildew affects open-ground plants more severely in dry than in wet weather. Outbreaks are usually associated with warmer weather and are recognised by a powdery white coating occurring in patches or covering the leaves, shoots and inflorescence. In the alpine house, the disease is responsible for damage to relatively few plants, although *Myosotis*, many of the Ranunculaceae and several members of the Leguminosae (*Lupinus* being the most significant) are susceptible.

What seems to be almost an offshoot of this ailment but is classified as Crucifer White Blister, is a nuisance that visits itself on the woolly-leaved *Draba* species in particular, progressing from small white pustules on the undersides of the leaves to a more generalised covering of the rosette and – since it is active even in late winter/early spring – the developing flower buds. Control measures normally involve the destruction of infected plants: unpleasant advice with a cushion of ten or more years standing, and possibly overly severe, for removal of the affected areas and replacement of the surface dressing can on occasion save the day.

Cushion plants occasionally succumb to a localised **wilting** that routinely affects first a few rosettes before spreading to affect the whole plant in a matter of perhaps a fortnight, notably in the warmer months of the year. Something similar is known in carnation crops, where **fusarium wilt** produces comparable chlorosis in a very small area but spreads rapidly: here the pathogen is soil borne and is usually introduced via infected material from another source. The genus *Dionysia* is prone to this trouble, and since at least one species of *Fusarium* is known to affect other Primulaceae (*Cyclamen* being the best-known host) it may well be that this offers a lead, although the suggestion is open to conjecture. Various species of fungus and bacteria are known to produce similar symptoms, characterised by the damage being confined to the aerial portions of the plant. Knocking a stricken plant out of its pot, the root system is usually quite unaffected.

To complicate the identification, however, broadly similar effects may be apparent in response to **root and foot rots**, found when soil temperatures are high and variously signalled by reduced growth, yellowing of the outer leaves and shrivelling of the shoots. In seedlings and young plants, the disease is known as damping off, and indicates unfavourable growing conditions – specifically overwatering or acid soils.

Lastly one might make mention of the numerous **rusts** that vary in importance from those that lead to limited defoliation (aquilegias under glass sometimes lose their leaves early because of rust attack, but rarely suffer a fatal attack) to those that despatch their victims, as with campanulas affected by Coltsfoot Rust, and the few Andean *Nototriche* that have come into contact with Hollyhock Rust.

Methods of control

Increasingly there is a movement away from the 'reflex action' use of chemicals to control any incidence of pest or disease attack. The first line of defence is to eliminate as far as possible any potential sources of trouble: weeds in the vicinity of the alpine house likely to support pathogens that can transfer to other plants; introducing new plants without checking thoroughly for signs of any malady; insufficient ventilation leading to either fungal diseases or (especially in the summer) soaring temperatures and scorch; the prompt removal of any damaged tissue and (although this is not always practicable) dead foliage.

Having said this, one should admit that pests have developed the ingenuity to exploit almost any niche, and controlling the environment to repulse one can encourage another. The manipulation of both the temperature and humidity of the glasshouse in particular is a very involved subject, but in general it can be stated that at lower temperatures, and in certain conditions (a cool night following on from a warm day) relative humidity can quickly rise until dewpoint is reached, whereupon droplets of water condense on all available surfaces – glass, benching, plunge and plants. Fungal spores begin to germinate somewhat below this level, and it is wise to avoid such conditions by supplementing the ventilation and, in the wintertime, making sure that water is applied cautiously rather than according to a fixed routine.

In practice, however, the wise gardener will combat pests and diseases by a combination of deterrence and judicious application of chemical agents when other alternatives are exhausted. There are several very good reasons for such a regime, quite apart from the sheer cost of pesticides. Continuous application of the same chemicals can lead to the development of resistant strains – this has been the case with some red spider mite populations, for instance, where a programme of spraying that alternates the application of two different materials is recommended. Most pesticides can be subdivided into groups based around the different chemicals they comprise, and their gruesome means of control (tract poisons, suffocating agents and so on) serve to vary the attack.

A potential setback here is that the alternative may prove phytotoxic, even if the manufacturer's instructions regarding the rate of dilution and compatibility are followed to the letter. Alpines seldom if ever figure in the trials carried out to identify susceptible plants, and as such it is bad practice to blanket spray an entire collection or indeed a one and only specimen except when the plant is likely to die if left untreated. Cheshunt compound, a long-established control for damping-off diseases, is now known to be incompatible with some genera, dimethoate can damage the foliage of a wide range of plants, *Cyclamen* included, and some alpines are sensitive to a wide range of chemicals. Those whose dense growth attracts pests – *Calceolaria*, *Viola* and *Soldanella* come to mind – pose a particular problem, and for these the compounds based on derris and pyrethrum offer the best alternative.

A further consideration is the danger these chemicals pose to the user, for whilst most of us are wary in our handling of them, the measuring out and transfer from bottle to applicator provide opportunities for unwelcome contact. In the face of evidence that materials like HCH (lindane) are carcinogenic, the confined space of a greenhouse seems no place to be wandering with a pressure spray dispensing these invariably nauseating and foul-smelling sprays.

For day-to-day purposes, the use-and-throw-away aerosols are perfectly adequate, providing a finer mist than the most delicately adjusted spray. They offer a quick and convenient means of dealing with localised outbreaks and, unlike concentrates that have to be used in often confusing ratios of pesticide to water and administered used soon after mixing, they deliver exactly the quantity required with no fear of botching the dilution instructions.

It seems fairly pointless to list the various chemicals in use – most pesticides are sold under tradenames, and by the time one had read through the small print and arrived at the active ingredient contained, the question of suitability has usually been answered. The legislation on which chemicals are available for amateur use is still in a state of change. The most important point to ascertain is whether they have a persistent effect or are intended to have only a contact action, in which latter case care must be taken to spray the underside of the leaves and any other inaccessible but afflicted areas. Other pesticides leave a residue that continues to protect after the initial trouble has cleared, and with plants that persistently succumb to a particular ailment, some gardeners feel it necessary to innoculate with a systemic pesticide, which is taken up into the sap and continues to repel attacks over a period measured in weeks, perhaps months.

Alpines in their winter resting period may object to a drenching spray, and a further method worth considering is the use of dusts, normally dispensed in puffer packs, which the operator squeezes gently, hoping to eject just enough of the powder to coat the affected area lightly. HCH, despite the earlier stricture, is very useful for curbing aphid infestations in this form, and whilst some people dislike the unsightly covering that it provides until new growth takes over, green sulphur remains a very effective fungicide that often works where more recent materials such as benomyl have failed.

It is, of course, quite possible to fumigate the entire glasshouse, either by igniting the vapour cones stocked by nurseries and garden centres, or by installing an electrical vaporiser. In both cases, the foliage of the plants to be treated needs to be reasonably dry, since the particles released are in some instances phytotoxic when they meet with water. Assuming that a power cable has been provided, then an electrical fumigator is a more convenient device: those on the market are supplied with a fixing bracket and work by containing a reservoir of the pesticide near to a heating element which vaporises on contact. Placed at bench height midway along the structure, one unit will – depending on the model – prove effective over an area of up to 1,000 cubic metres. The best plan is to close down the alpine house in the late evening, possibly sealing any area where the fumes might escape (such as the door frame) and then ventilate thoroughly before entering the next morning. With contact pesticides, a second application will be necessary a week or so later. Otherwise, newly emerged pests that withstood the earlier dose in pupae or egg form can restart the old trouble.

Some chemicals can be utilised to give a specific control, such as pirimicarb, which is toxic to aphids but does not kill other insects and makes possible an integrated system of biological control. This age-old concept does not provide the complete answer in our experience, but the methods involved are improving and widening all the time. It is now possible to send off and obtain through the post a sachet of the microscopic predator *Phytoseiulus persimilis* which limits numbers of red spider mites (more so when the plants are pot-thick, i.e. when the plant pots are touching). Work on a fungal pathogen of aphids and a species of nematode that is parasitic on vine weevil grubs has progressed well, and these will shortly be available to amateur gardeners.

Reading through this catalogue of ills, one might be forgiven for thinking that the odds are stacked against success. Luckily this is not so; having diagnosed the problem there are usually several methods of containing it, and the intelligent use of the thumb and forefinger will stem all manner of ills.

Cleanliness

Keeping the alpine house in good order has a dual function. In the first place prompt and continual action will work against the establishment of the pathogens. A number of the higher alpines are unused to the overcrowding of the average collection, and under such unnatural conditions drips from cracked glass, mouldering clusters of dead foliage and poor light transmission can all invite secondary problems. Most owners see the structure not simply as a growing area but an integral part of the garden and a display unit. It is obvious that general untidiness is not conducive to these aims. Clinical standards of hygiene may be applicable to individual plants at certain times of the year, but before dealing with this consideration, what of the general structure?

Inside and out
During the course of the growing season, the glass panes gradually acquire a film of dust and other air-borne deposits: it has been estimated that on average 10 per cent of the available light will be blocked in this way after just six weeks in urban areas. One doubts that the build-up continues at this rate but several times a year it is advisable to clean the outer surfaces. A soft-bristled yard brush provides the suitable reach. Before commencing, make sure that the drainpipe is not discharging soapy effluent from this operation into your water butt. Polishing the glass with a cloth is all very well, but horticultural glass is frequently sent out with the edges still very sharp, and where they overlap an over-enthusiastic sweep can cut through the cloth and cause lacerations to the hand.

The inner surface of the glass is less affected by dirt, but spiders' webs are soon spun that look rather unsightly, and moss often lodges where the glazing bar and glass meet, especially where the roof and sides join. Pests often overwinter in similar positions, and it is sensible to tackle the problem in mid autumn, for preference before the weather breaks and makes moving the plants to temporary quarters an awkward job. There are several disinfectants on the market that can be used without their fumes harming the plants – read the manufacturer's instructions and, if toxic products are used, leave the alpine house empty for 24 hours to allow harmful vapours to disperse. Removing the plants whilst this is done is a major task and, without a second glass-covered area in which to put them, in most cases is simply not practicable, so the greenhouse cleaning agents on the market, none of them phytotoxic at any stage of use, are usually worth the extra expense involved. Choose a well-lit breezy day for preference, to allow the interior to dry off before nightfall.

At the same time, it is helpful to remove the pots, one bench (or section) at a time, cleaning the staging and plunge material before checking each pot, scrubbing it clean and returning it to the bench. This is a counsel of perfection, but once a year should be sufficient, bearing in mind that quite a few of the plants are likely to have been repotted earlier in the year, when a similar procedure was carried out.

The staging itself may need attention – wooden benching needs coating with a preservative once every two or three years and even aluminium corrodes. It does so in the form of a white power which speckles the surface, and whilst not threatening in the short term, it is best to clean all traces off with a scouring pad, painting a zinc chromate primer onto the affected areas.

Whether the pots are fully plunged or simply rested on a surface of chippings, growth of mosses and liverwort is almost unavoidable. Preparations claimed to kill these growths are not altogether effective (and have a harmful effect on several genera, *Orchis*, *Meconopsis* and *Ramonda* among them), so the best course of action is to scoop off and discard any matted areas of the surface layer, stirring the top few centimetres and spraying with a weak dose of a disinfectant suitable for garden use. At this stage any dead leaves or pests brought to the surface by the activity can be dealt with.

Clay pots that spend their time up to the rim in a sand plunge are kept relatively clean by their surround, and only the top few centimetres require attention, but free-standing pots soon gain a surface layer of moss, or become unsightly through the encrustations that coat their sides. Several pests have the habit of laying eggs either on the side of the container or, more usually, around the drainage hole, so the operation is not merely a cosmetic one.

Traditionally this chore was carried out with a scrubbing brush, a bucket of water and, optionally, coarse silver sand to act as a scarifying agent. Anyone who has attempted this will realise that the handler, and worse still the plants, quickly tend to acquire a spattering of muddy water. Moreover, few brushes can be successfully manipulated around the rim of the pot, and handling becomes difficult with the smaller sizes.

Nowadays, the process is more easily completed using the soap-impregnated pads of wire wool sold for general household purposes. Resist the temptation to use even tepid water – which leads to an over-abundance of soapsuds – and finish off by cleansing the area with a damp cloth. The worst pots to deal with are those where limestone chippings have been used in the compost or as a topdressing, and here it may prove easier to rehouse the plant in a fresh pot, soak the old one and scrub thoroughly with the worry of damaging the plant removed.

This is perhaps the place to say that reserves of clay pots should not (as one sometimes observes) be stored with an untidy clutter of labels, bottles of insecticide and discarded foliage under the bench. The best place is a frost-free shed or garage, with shelving supported by the strongest brackets possible . . . just one 16cm pot can weigh over 1kg when empty, and the combined weight of a collection needs to be borne in mind. With the much lighter plastic pots, stability is the only argument against stacking them vertically, but with the clay version, where those sold in any one size are stored one inside the other, it is important to lay them on their sides. Whether hand thrown or machine cast, each will vary fractionally, and upright storage will have the effect of clamping them inextricably together.

The plants themselves

In their natural habitat, the plants receive very little in the way of grooming, save the haphazard pruning of herbivores and the withering and dispersal of dead leaves by strong winds. Seed capsules may persist from previous seasons, whole branches or sections of a cushion die away in response to drought or when damaged in a rockfall, and in some cases seedlings will grow up and flourish not just around but even through their parent's corpse.

For the alpine house owner, however, the very different conditions prevailing and aesthetic requirements combine to make a continual tidying operation very worthwhile. It is a less straightforward matter than might be imagined, because not all plants appreciate the removal of dead foliage at the first opportunity, and of those that do, some are far more predisposed to fungal diseases than others.

Before examining the foliage, we should stop to look at the topdressing, which can quickly moss over, whilst liverwort adds to the problems. Moss that spreads to infiltrate a cushion plant is particularly awkward to remove, so early action is necessary – the same goes for liverwort where the plant involved spreads by slender runners, too brittle to withstand forcible separation. The most useful tool is a small metal spatula, channelled and tapering almost to a point at one end, which is generally referred to as a 'widger'. This will easily gouge away affected areas, which are quick to form where the plant in question is surface rooting and needs the uppermost layer of compost kept moist. Conversely, with some plants it is worth buying sphagnum moss from the florist and using this as a topdressing, both to maintain humidity and discourage liverwort. Orchids from damper regions – the Himalayan pleiones for example, grow well treated in this way, and I have seen *Shortia* and *Ramonda* responding well to similar treatment. Stray seedlings often appear at the edge of a pot, and these need removing either when repotting or at an early stage, before their root systems become too tangled with the main plant to permit an easy transfer. With a little experience it is easy to distinguish them from the commoner weeds that infiltrate, either carried on the wind or imported with unsterilised compost.

When it comes to the plant itself, it is not always easy to be certain that the

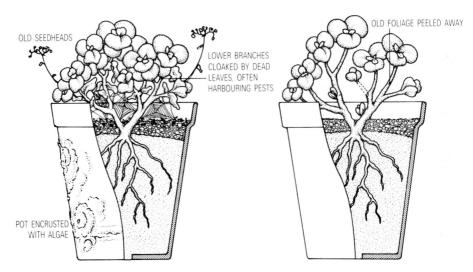

OLD SEEDHEADS

LOWER BRANCHES
CLOAKED BY DEAD
LEAVES, OFTEN
HARBOURING PESTS

OLD FOLIAGE PEELED AWAY

POT ENCRUSTED
WITH ALGAE

Figure 6   A pot plant before cleaning   *Figure 7   A pot plant after cleaning*

part to be removed is actually dead. Many shoots will be obscured by dead leaf bases and the growing tip, encased in this material, is prone to removal by overzealous cleaning. Some autumn-flowering plants present an equally untidy appearance that hides the new flowerbuds, a good example being the Greek *Allium callimischon*. Other plants have foliage that shrivels away in dry conditions but can be revitalised when the rains come. All the ramondas behave in this fashion – the rule is that if the leaf can be pulled away easily (usually as new growth starts in the spring) then it is truly dead, otherwise leave well alone.

The need to remove dead foliage is greatest in late autumn when the cold, frequently damp nights can soon lead to the growth of botrytis on the lifeless leaves. Relatively few plants shed their leaves completely and whilst it is generally only those species with larger leaves that need an annual cleansing, not infrequently just one or two rosettes will die and require prompt removal. Again, no leaf is detached until it can be removed with a gentle downward tug. This is stressed because in hot weather some leaves may discolour badly, turning a pale yellow green or sustaining damage at the margin, but continue to function during this period. If removal is attempted too early it is easy to leave behind a snag of the petiole, which may act as a focus for disease. On the other hand, any flowers (and capsules where seed is not required) are cleared away as they fade, which often leads, particularly with *Campanula*, to a second crop of flowers. New growth can make the fruiting body hard to pinpoint, so if seed is required it is probably best to leave a thin scattering of seedheads around the periphery of the plant.

In general, tidying the old growth is a job for fingers rather than a penknife or similar, which can easily slip and sever a shoot, but when dealing with toughened leaf bases or excising a damaged area, an ordinary pair of scissors, together with the small but long-handled variety sold for surgical purposes, will be found useful.

Shrubby plants, where each branch terminates in a resting bud, need least pruning: by autumn the flower buds for the following year have in many cases already set, and if it is felt necessary to trim in the interests of a better shape, then early summer is a more suitable time, providing the option of using the severed material for cuttings. Dormant growth buds further back along the stem will invariably awaken with this treatment, but a piecemeal approach is recommended. Cutting into old wood is not always successful, and traditionally temperamental genera like *Daphne* are sometimes badly damaged by such attempts.

A second class of sub-shrubby alpines form a woody trunk that branches out with age, and the deciduous foliage usually needs clipping away down to the level of the dormant crowns. The danger lies with those plants which form new growth almost before the old year is out, like *Viola cazorlensis*, where the old leaves help to prevent frosting. Plants from the higher mountains – *Paraquilegia anemonoides*, for example – will often awaken at the same time, but are more resilient against low temperatures. Where flowering takes place from the current year's growth, then hard pruning can often help to rejuvenate a plant: without this treatment, the overall structure may begin to open out and the old shoots become spindly and brittle.

It is probable, though, that many of the plants grown will be evergreen, with the amount of dead foliage influenced by the severity of the winter. If the plant forms a loose mat, then taking off the spent basal leaves is often advisable to discourage fungal attack – most of the European high alpine *Viola* respond to this treatment. But if the leaves are packed tightly into rosettes, or are particularly small, then it is often not practicable to clear them away. One has to rely on good ventilation to prevent stagnant moisture lingering around the dormant shoots, dusting those few species that regularly succumb to disease with a fungicide in powder form.

Despite these precautions, sometimes rosettes will wither away or become infected with botrytis following on from moisture condensing on the alpine house roof, and perhaps dripping onto the plants. Unless remedied in the very early stages, it is usually necessary to remove the affected portion in its entirety, cutting back to sound growth and checking that the adjoining areas are not damaged. With cushion plants, any undesirable moisture can be removed by carefully patting sheets of paper kitchen towel onto the damp surface and snipping out any diseased rosettes rather than pulling them away with tweezers, an action which can dislodge healthy material when performed by any but the most dextrous of hands. Carefully adding a little more topdressing, or sliding a rock fragment beneath the cushion, is normally sufficient to close the gap created, and the idea of filling the holes with gravel finds little favour nowadays. Only where it can be seen that the cushion roots as it goes, relying not simply on a system that depends from the main neck but sending down other roots adventitiously from within the topgrowth, is it worth working dry silver sand into the hole, before proceeding as above.

Bulbous plants sometimes exhibit damage to their leaf tips where a cold snap catches the well-developed overwintering shoots but although unsightly, it is not necessary to remove damaged tips except for exhibition purposes. If attempted, it may well be better not to cut into the undamaged tissue but choose the area immediately above the base of the scar, otherwise further dieback tends to occur. More important is the removal of spent flowers, particularly in the case of species like *Iris nicolai*, *Sternbergia candida* and certain of the *Narcissus* that bloom during the winter when grown in lowland gardens. Generally unhealthy foliage is invariably a sign that the bulb itself is under stress. Carefully excavating down to the root area, using a 'widger', sometimes shows that the compost is too dry, in which case the yellowing leaves are the result of premature dormancy, and apart from a slightly small bulb next year the consequences are seldom serious. At other times, investigation shows that the bulb has rotted because the compost was (1) too wet or (2) frozen solid; treatments that even the hardiest bulbs normally resent. Usually it is enough to discard the damaged bulbs and surrounding soil, dust the remainder with benomyl or similar, and replace with fresh, just-moist compost. Some genera, particularly *Erythronium* and *Narcissus*, begin to grow in mid summer, and withholding water to restrain growth is generally harmful, but those from semi-desert habitats – and especially the Oncocyclus iris – can be kept dry until the end of autumn, which discourages early leaf growth.

6. A typical alpine house arrangement

7. A close-up of a *Lewisia* collection

8. Short-lived species such as *Campanula alpina* are often easily raised from seed

9. *Oncocyclus iris* appreciate the extra headroom

8 Plants in Pots

This is by far the most popular method of alpine house gardening. A wide range of plants can be fitted into a relatively small space, varying the collection and drafting in others from the frames and plunge beds in accordance with their relative flowering periods. For anyone hoping to exhibit their plants, this arrangement is more or less indispensable, but many enthusiasts to whom this does not apply still choose to pot up their plants.

A pot allows us to provide radically different growing conditions for plants positioned only a few feet apart, and move them to more congenial quarters as the year progresses. Should a plant become diseased or host to some pest, it can be removed before the trouble spreads to neighbouring plants: time and again one sees a zoning effect where infection has been allowed to spread. Obviously the closer the pots are arranged together, the greater the likelihood of cross infection. There is – or should be – a relative orderliness about growing plants in pots: their boundaries are checked so that they do not spread into one another, as is so often seen in the wild, and the system encourages individual attention. It also implies fairly continuous attention. The notion that plants so housed thrive on neglect is usually self-deluding, and it is regular monitoring that probably leads to the arguable conclusion that some alpines do better if pot grown.

The pot itself

In their early years, most alpines grow well enough in plastic pots – they may well out-perform their rivals, since drying out takes place less rapidly and they can easily be kept scrupulously clean, which minimises the risk of disease. The observation that many seedlings germinate with snowmelt, and therefore are equipped to form a root system quickly in moist soil, fits in with this behaviour. As they age, water may still be needed in quantity, but its application generally has to be more precise, and this is why 'thirsty' plants such as *Soldanella* that will tolerate continuous moisture are often said to grow better in plastic pots. Providing a grittier, very well-aerated compost helps, but there is limited support for growing alpines in plastic pots much over 15cm diameter.

Concern was expressed that the traditional unglazed terracotta flowerpot

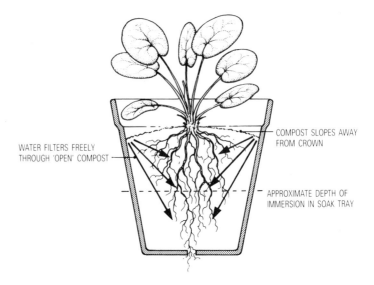

WATER FILTERS FREELY
THROUGH 'OPEN' COMPOST

COMPOST SLOPES AWAY
FROM CROWN

APPROXIMATE DEPTH OF
IMMERSION IN SOAK TRAY

Figure 8   Full size clay plant pot

would soon be a thing of the past, but the present trend confirms a resurgence in its use. Several manufacturers produce them on a large scale and, in England at least, a number of smaller potteries either produce a range already or will do so to order. Elsewhere, enthusiasts have gone to the lengths of setting up a kiln and making pots to their own specifications where no alternative supply exists.

Aesthetic considerations aside, the chief advantage of a clay flowerpot is its porosity, which allows for both the steady absorption of moisture if plunged and, since water can evaporate from any exposed surfaces or slowly leach through the potwall, a degree of regulation not possible with the plastic alternative. Various figures are given for the difference in soil temperature between comparable clay and plastic pots, but it is clear that clay pots provide a cooler root run, particularly in the daytime, and this too can help with the cultivation of many alpines.

The question of breakages is always raised, and certainly a proportion of clay pots can be written off each year, either through incorrect storage, frost-shattering or their owners clumsiness. The appreciable weight of each pot, combined with differences in any one batch, let alone a given size (especially if they are hand thrown rather than machine made), mean that if stacked vertically they lock together. Take a look in a well-ordered potting shed and you will generally find a series of sturdy shelves, with the pots neatly graded by size, lying on their sides with their rims facing outwards for ease of selection. It is a sensible discipline never to leave so-called 'dead' pots (where the plant has departed) underneath the staging but to maintain cleanliness by dealing with it immediately, if only because the dry incrustations of compost and limescale are nigh inpossible to remove in their entirety.

Losses through frosting can be severe in a hard winter, and are even more damaging to the plant if the fragments fall away to expose the roots to intense cold. The larger sizes are usually worst affected, the more so if the compost is moist when the freezing occurs, since the greater body of soil expands as its water content freezes, exerting greater force with inevitable consequences. The very porosity that generally works to our advantage means that internal stresses can shatter any exposed portion – i.e. the pot rim, which often forms a thicker, 3–6cm deep border, although many of the older designs do not incorporate this feature. Much depends on the composition of the baked clay, for I am still using pots made at least 30 years ago, whereas more recent supplies have varied greatly in quality.

The actual dimensions of the pots sold differ considerably, even when choosing a standard flowerpot, quite apart from the several depths and shapes sometimes seen. The idea is to make the plant the focus of attention, so few will entertain these models moulded into the shape of seashells or crested in some fashion. Also rejected are the shallow, purportedly 'alpine' pans that are useful to the *Sempervivum* specialist and virtually no one else.

For the same reason, the smaller sizes of half pots are of only limited value. The high proportion of root to topgrowth is one of the most obvious features of many alpines, and the speed with which the roots travel to the bottom of the pot and through the drainage hole, irrespective of whether the compost is kept reasonably moist, makes root damage a perpetual likelihood. It is repeatedly the case that a plant will first concentrate its efforts on establishing itself, spreading little but building up a substantial root system, before increasing its girth by suckers, lateral growths or stolons, and since downward root growth is often more marked than outward expansion, a deeper pot is appropriate.

After a period of absence, the 'long tom' flowerpot is making a comeback, and if it does not always look sightly when exhibited (the proportion of pot to

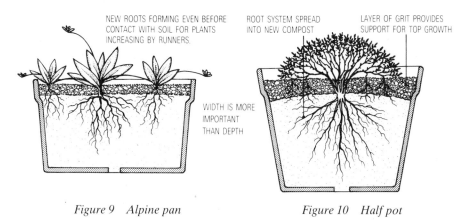

Figure 9   Alpine pan   Figure 10   Half pot

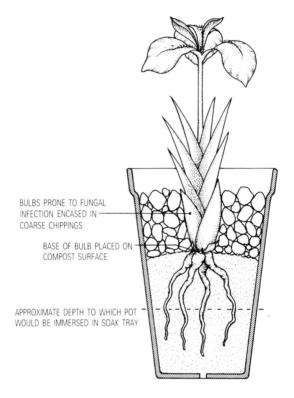

BULBS PRONE TO FUNGAL
INFECTION ENCASED IN
COARSE CHIPPINGS

BASE OF BULB PLACED ON
COMPOST SURFACE

APPROXIMATE DEPTH TO WHICH POT
WOULD BE IMMERSED IN SOAK TRAY

Figure 11   Long tom

plant appears excessive), this feature is irrelevant when it is plunged. It is always said that their particular advantage is in accommodating the extensive roots of plants like *Anchusa caespitosa* and the majority of the *Oncocyclus* species of *Iris*, or deep-seated corms such as those of *Erythronium* that are invariably pulled by their contractile roots 10cm or more below the surface. The genuine article tapers slightly and is some one and a half times as deep as its maximum diameter. The larger sizes are very scarce, and in their place we now see increasing quantities of the so-called 'chimney pot', straight sided and usually thicker than the long tom, but very useful when growing plants that would naturally inhabit crevices, and are accustomed to their roots following a narrow channel. *Daphne petraea* 'Grandiflora', for example, is a popular choice.

Separate from the necessity of encompassing extensive roots, the depth of the container also guarantees better drainage and, in consequence, the air-filled porosity of the compost. What should be examined, however, for this feature to be exploited, is the size of the drainage hole, which is periodically inadequate for the pot size. The knitting-needle-sized holes often seen are of little use, requiring the gardener to chip very carefully at the edge of the hole, aiming inwards to minimise the number of pots broken during the conversion.

The smallest pots available have a diameter of 5cm and are really only appropriate for tiny seedlings or cuttings of slow-growing plants. The largest size in general use is 30cm across, which can be attributed to tradition rather than any particular logic. There is still a vestigial dislike for large specimens of what are characterised as small and delicate plants, and the show schedules of several societies stipulate this upper limit for single plants. Cases of people dividing up the plant, planting it out or even discarding it once this size has been reached are not unusual.

It is desirable to have a range of pot sizes between these two limits, but no real need to have reserves across the whole span. Certain sizes are more useful than others, and the likelihood is that 6.5cm, 9cm and 16cm pots will be in greatest demand. The number of alpines that will progress happily through these three sizes without the need for any intermediates far outweighs those few that have to move up warily with a bare minimum of extra legroom. If the pots are plunged, it is far easier when repotting to move the new batch of 9cm and 16cm models into the already established holes of those which have in turn been potted up a size or two, or placed in a plunge bed outdoors.

No collection of pot plants is static, and unless the owner is so inept that they have to be replaced annually, the space available progressively diminishes. Reorganising the benches to accommodate one or two extra pots can be a logistic nightmare, and a modest degree of standardisation is a help.

Pot meets plant

It seems to me that untutored growers are more diffident about the act of moving a plant from one pot to another than almost any other aspect of the hobby. Why else does one see plants left for years in the same pot as they arrived in from the nursery, or the process delayed long beyond the stage at which action would have been appropriate? To make matters worse, many texts have emphasised the supposedly catastrophic effects of root disturbance on numerous alpine house plants, implying that attempts at repotting often fail. This is unfortunate and misleading. Whilst no one could claim an unblemished record, there are a number of steps that can be taken to minimise damage to the plant in what is admittedly a periodically difficult operation. Normally writers distinguish between potting up, potting on, repotting and resoiling, but the basic actions are much the same. It is simply that larger plants are more unwieldly to handle, and if elderly may take longer to recover from the effects of any damage that results.

The first essential is to have a clear and well-lit working area, and it has to be said that the commercially produced potting benches, designed to fit into the greenhouse benching system, are seldom adequate. Not only do they waste valuable space that could otherwise be utilised for growing more plants, but they are made too small for their purpose – presumably to try to overcome the first objection.

Nurserymen tend to have matters better organised, using a separate potting shed with lighting and a tap – facilities often absent from the alpine house itself. A long bench area at table height can easily be wiped down (the rim on the specially designed models prevents this) and the materials can be kept close at hand, rather than laboriously ferried in. I have seen garages and conservatories partially given over to this purpose, whilst in some tolerant households the kitchen fulfils all but the last criterion, compensated for by the proximity of the coffee or teapot.

Having dispensed with these basic matters, there remains the sequence of events associated with installing a plant in a new pot, which here follows a five-point plan.

1 When to repot

The general rule is to wait until the plant shows obvious signs of requiring a larger pot, usually when roots begin to extend from the drainage hole. This will mean that the plant is in active growth, and gives a fairly wide option (depending on the local climate), although there is more risk with autumn replantings, which may not have taken hold before winter sets in.

Gardeners who live in areas that experience very warm summer weather often wish to avoid this period. The plant may well already be under stress after its move, and broad-leaved species (numerous primulas for example) will usually wilt if moved then, the leaves losing more water than can be replaced by the roots. Seedlings prior to flowering are less vulnerable. It is normal to repot summer-flowering alpines in the early spring, soon after their growth has recommenced, whereas most spring-flowering species are left until after flowering, when their spurt of new growth is not normally checked if care is taken to keep the compost moist. Plants whose new leaves are easily bruised or otherwise damaged, *Primula allionii* being an obvious example, are best left until early autumn, by which time the foliage will have matured and can withstand handling.

However, it may be necessary to disturb a pot plant 'out of season' if it is ailing, as the only means of determining the nature of the problem. This may reveal that the roots have failed to grow into the new compost following repotting, or possibly pest damage (vine weevils are a menace in this respect). The difficulty of deciding whether the apparent malaise is a normal feature of the plant's annual growth cycle can complicate the decision to investigate further, but in general there is little to be said for leaving an unhealthy plant in the same pot in the vague hope of a return to prime conditon. Often a plant that makes comparatively little root growth will grow happily for a year or two, then suffer an insidious decline as the fertility and structure of the compost change. Others form congested crowns that benefit from division every few years – if this is not done the older, central portion frequently dies away, leaving the young peripheral growths marooned around the edge of the pot. Many of the more exacting campanulas (*C. cenisia*, *C. excisa*, *C. piperi* and *C. shetleri*) are affected in this way, as are many of the European, high alpine violas (*V. calcarata*, *V. cenisia* and *V. diversifolia* among them).

Nearly all the plants that retire underground for the summer suffer least disturbance if repotted towards the end of their dormant period. They *can* be moved in full growth, but the risk of a check in growth increases. This is especially true of plants with an unbranched root system of annual duration, which may be incapable of regeneration if damage occurs, leading to an untimely early dormancy. Many will benefit from annual renewal of the compost, and since there is no topgrowth to worry about, they can easily be tipped out, graded if necessary, and replanted in a clean pot, often of the same size. At this stage, the non-flowering-size offsets (if any) are potted up separately, effecting a ready means of increase.

A minority only flower well after they have built up a loose cluster of bulbs or fleshy scales, which come adrift at the slightest knock and take several years to regenerate a flowering-size group. This phenomenon is encountered among some narcissus (many clones of *N. fernandesii*, *N. jonquilla* and *N. willkommii*) and a few North American fritillarias (*F. affinis*, *F. recurva*, etc.). To avoid loss of flowering the dry compost is carefully scraped away with a 'widger' down to the level of the base of the bulbs, and fresh compost replaced to the depth of the old.

2 Off with the old

The trickiest aspect of potting is to extricate the plant without leaving half the compost (and roots) disembodied and stuck fast in the old pot, or finding that after a considerable tussle the whole comes away at the least expected moment, leaving the plant upended on the potting bench with the shoots splayed under the weight of the compost. Two pairs of hands may be preferable, but the roles assigned to either operator need to be agreed in advance if sharp words and recriminations are to be avoided.

First the preparatory work. Any fully developed flowers are usually removed, and awkwardly projecting or otherwise unwanted shoots trimmed away. These make useful propagating material, and it is strongly recommended that before repotting a one and only specimen of *any* unusual plant, attempts should be made to grow on at least one potential replacement.

Next the pot is tilted slightly and any topdressing taken away. This is of great importance if large pieces of slate or other rock have been incorporated, which would otherwise slice through or jolt against the topgrowth come the final push. However, without the support of the topdressing, the tight cushion form of some plants gives way to a collapsed, lolling collection of columnar branches, and an ingenious solution has been to hold them together temporarily with a section of nylon stocking, which can be stretched under the base, over the dome and secured at the side nearest the handler. Stoloniferous plants can be more difficult still – the gravel topdressing is loosely bound by the network of often fragile runners, and some pieces will unavoidably become severed,

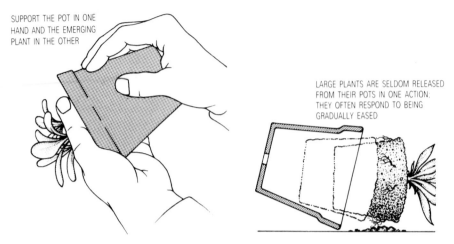

SUPPORT THE POT IN ONE HAND AND THE EMERGING PLANT IN THE OTHER

LARGE PLANTS ARE SELDOM RELEASED FROM THEIR POTS IN ONE ACTION: THEY OFTEN RESPOND TO BEING GRADUALLY EASED

Figure 12   Unpotting a young plant   *Figure 13   Unpotting an established plant*

although the suckering habit normally guarantees that new growth will arise lower down the damaged stems.

What happens after that depends much upon the size of the pot and the degree to which the plant is potbound. Ideally, the roots will not have travelled far beyond the drainage hole, but now and again when the pot is lifted, a clinging mass of root and plunge material will be suspended beneath. It is usually best to sever this, although if root disturbance is likely to be resented, there is partial aid to hand by washing off the sand/grit and judging whether the roots that remain will slither through the drainage hole when repotting takes place.

Small plastic pots are malleable, and if the first firm knock against the side of the potting bench does not free the rootball, a gentle manipulation of the rim can often help. But with clay pots, another strategy is called for. It is said that the recurrent nuisance of the compost adhering to the pot sides is caused by using a pot in a damp state when repotting, which seems rather dubious. Earthenware varies in its porosity, and it is far more likely that the more porous containers attract roots to their moisture reserve . . . often a dense, felt-like inner coating results, which has to be removed when repotting occurs.

The orthodox procedure is to tap the basal edge of the pot smartly against a hard surface once or twice, turn it to face away from you and slightly downwards, tap the rim sharply and bring one hand to support the now free contents, with the other pulling away the pot. A small rootball will rest quite happily on the inner blade of a trowel. With the larger pot sizes, it is better first to ensure the roots and compost are loose from the pot side, then partially withdraw the pot before using both hands to cradle the rootball, bringing it to rest on a mound of compost.

Not always does the parting of pot and plant go smoothly at the first attempt, and it is increasingly common to find that before the separation is effected, a round-bladed knife is carefully run around the edge. This is all very well, but with plants that send out shoots to the sides of the pot, severing of some of the growth is likely. This technique presumably takes its cue from the kitchen, where much the same dodge prevents cakes from sticking in their baking tins.

Ideally, the compost should be moist but not wet when repotting takes place. Too wet and it is difficult to separate from the roots without causing them to break; too dry and the rootball can disintegrate. Another consideration: unless the newly installed plant and pot are soaked in a water trough, the old compost and therefore the roots do not always take up water from the damp surround of the new if inserted in an already dry state. When the plant fails, it is commonly found that the dry, hard plug of old compost has failed to take up any moisture, and the plant has died of drought.

If the plant is potbound, it is sound practice to tease out some of the larger roots, spreading them carefully over the new compost. Some damage will result, but can be lessened in many cases by standing the rootball in shallow water, which generally serves to loosen the tight coil that often develops at the base.

3 Tidying up

With the plant out of its pot, an opportunity exists to carry out any pruning or shaping before carrying on to the next stage. This may prove unnecessary, but it is always worth checking the general condition of the plant whilst the chance to examine both top and root growth exists. If this is likely to take any length of time, it is advisable to cover the roots to avoid drying out – with larger plants I use an old teatowel, moistened and then wrung out.

Some ailments are awkward to diagnose without exposing the roots: root aphids, for instance, contribute to a general decline in the plant's health, but depending upon the severity of the attack are not always apparent at the level of the crown visible to casual observation. Root rots too can be revealed in the process, and carefully cutting out the affected area (discarding the compost at the same time) is the recommended measure.

When it comes to the topgrowth, the most frequent need is to clear away moss and liverwort growth, which quite apart from being unsightly can smother new shoots. The several algicides on the market do not suit every species, and are not always as effective as could be wished. In severe cases, it may be advisable to remove completely the top few centimetres of compost.

Any dead basal leaves or old flower stalks missed in the autumn can be peeled away cleanly, with the exception of cushion plants, where the large number of marcescent leaves and the impossibility of separating the numerous shoots makes this process impossible. Plants with brittle stems like *Linum elegans* will usually be found to have a number of broken or withered shoots which need snipping away, and sometimes a portion of a cushion plant will die off: without the pressure exerted by the topdressing, it is easier gently to part the surrounding healthy growth, and deftly sever the affected area prior to

63

repotting, when it will usually prove possible to push growth together and close up the gap. Be wary of tugging: healthy growth can be accidentally removed in this way.

Plants that have grown straggly with age – *Primula marginata* and *Helichrysum sibthorpii* are typical examples – are best pruned fairly hard at an earlier stage, waiting until the dormant vegetative buds further down the stems promote before disturbing the roots. But if just one or two 'leaders' have grown away, these can be safely removed at the repotting stage.

This is also the time to carry out division, discarding the weaker or damaged shoots that are left. It may be possible to split the crowns by merely shaking off the old compost and carefully pulling the required number of sections apart, but often more drastic action is required. Where the crowns do not fall apart naturally, but form a continuous mass with roots emanating from several points, it will be necessary to cut through the connecting tissue with a sharp knife, applying a fungicide to the affected surfaces. And if the growth is sufficiently open, two hand forks inserted back to back and levered against one another (a miniature version of the standard method in the herbaceous border) remains effective. Plants that do not object to some dampness around their 'neck' can be immersed in water up to this level, which with persistence will wash away much of the compost, making division very much easier.

Whichever means of division is chosen, the separated plants will require extra attention if they are to establish themselves. In particular, a cool position shaded from the midday sun is preferable, and the plants should be treated as newly rooted cuttings until new growth appears.

4 Rehousing

Before removing the plant from its old pot, it will be necessary to have to hand an adequate quantity of ready-mixed compost (large pots takes a surprising amount of filling, so check in advance to avoid running out of infill half way through) and a suitable container – though not necessarily the next size up. The growth rate of the plant normally determines this choice. For example *Androsace vandellii* is unlikely to increase by more than a few centimetres in any one year, although root growth can be disproportionate, requiring a full pot or long tom that provides an acceptable ratio of topgrowth to surface area. On the other hand, a surface rooting plant like *Lobelia linnaeoides* will spread quite quickly, and the choice lies between repeated repotting (perhaps four times in a single growing season) or a compromise by using a pot that looks slightly too wide. It is not usually desirable for the plant to overlap its pot, except in those instances where the post-flowering leaves expand rapidly before dying back to a central cluster of resting buds in the late autumn.

Years ago it was standard to cover the drainage holes with shards of broken pot and a thin layer of peat or leafmould to prevent the compost from consolidating in this region and impeding drainage. This practice has now largely died out – the high proportion of drainage material embodied in the compost makes it an irrelevance in most cases, but if the drainage hole is more than, say, a centimetre across, a single crock is an efficient means of preventing any compost from seeping out. Other solutions have their disadvantages. Perforated zinc is said to be toxic, although for many years I used small squares cut from a large sheet without noticing any harmfull effect. What led me to abandon this practice – a consideration that applies equally to plastic meshing – was the difficulty of extricating the roots once they had worked their way through this filter and out into the plunge material. Tap-rooted species would force their way through even the smallest gap, swelling again on the other side but constricted at the division, so that when moved they broke off all too easily. And a bottom layer of chippings 2cm deep with the larger pot sizes is still of some use in that the material falls away very readily when the plant is unpotted, exposing the root ends which can if necessary be unravelled somewhat to encourage the plant to grow into the fresh compost.

Whether the pot chosen is plastic or clay will naturally affect the subsequent watering pattern considerably, but there is little point in dictating that the two types cannot be mixed (except possibly with a self-watering system) when in practice few people possess enough glasshouse space to do otherwise. Since the watering requirements of each plant are assessed individually – albeit at speed – there is little enough reason for segregation, save perhaps in the owner's absence, when less experienced hands may be at the helm. At such times – holidays being the usual reason – specific advice in the form of concise notes affixed to each tray or section of bench ('only water if surface of compost feels dry', 'do not water pots where no foliage is visible', 'stand pot to half its depth in soak tray once a week' and so on) are of more practical use to an inexperienced caretaker than pages of advice that they will never have time to read, or a parting lecture on the theory of watering that will be quickly forgotten.

The new pot is measured alongside the waiting plant to gauge how much material can be put in the base for the roots to rest upon. Depending on the plant, it is generally desirable to pot it at the same level as before (at the junction of the upper roots and the caudex in most instances) or even slightly higher, sloping the compost surface away so that any overhead water drains to the margin of the pot rather than collecting at the neck. Other alpines are used to a progressive covering of loose scree material, and form roots at their nodes which anchor this steady topdressing. In cultivation they may appear rather etiolated, and benefit from a deeper planting, being careful to use a very sparse compost since natural drainage would invariably be very efficient. Numerous plants from the summer dry mountains of central Asia and the temperate Andes fall into this category – species increasingly seen in collections such as the dwarfer acantholimons, *Nassauvia lagascae* and *Chaetanthera villosa*.

Lowering the plant into its new quarters can prove awkward – it is nearly always preferable to centralise its final position, but delicate adjustments are best carried out once the rootball has been transferred safely, when coaxing with the fingers of one hand and the length of the widger controlled by the other

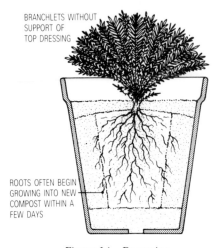

BRANCHLETS WITHOUT
SUPPORT OF
TOP DRESSING

ROOTS OFTEN BEGIN
GROWING INTO NEW
COMPOST WITHIN A
FEW DAYS

Figure 14   Repotting

determine the final position. Only if the plant has a very stout and woody neck, and the roots and compost are reasonably bound, should an attempt be made to lift it into position using the former as a convenient handhold . . . the risk of root and stock parting company can so easily be underestimated. Plants with foliage that is unpleasant to handle, being either spiny (*Erinacea anthyllis*, *Maihuenia poeppiggii* etc) or covered in stinging hairs (several species of *Loasa* and *Caiophora*) can sometimes be steered into position with a thin-pronged fork stabbed almost vertically into the compost on one side to steady the descent, and a piece of polythene stripping used as a sling which is pulled out from underneath when 'touchdown' has been achieved.

With smaller plants, where most of the compost will be off the roots, it is a straightforward matter of sprinkling the infill to the required level, perhaps lifting the neck once or twice to make sure the roots are not weighted in a mass at the base, but distributed widely, tapping the pot lightly to aid settlement and prevent air pockets. The latter can occur only too readily with larger plants, where it may not be possible to leave space between the plant and the inner pot wall to reach down with your fingertips and spread the compost. Here again a spatula-like device is required, which can be prodded to the bottom and moved round as the compost is added to ensure an even fill. The plant is warily levered backwards and forwards to prevent a shadow effect where the compost is caught at some point where root and pot touch. Although it can be a rather messy process, it may help to water in the plant stage by stage, which firms the compost without causing undue compaction. A trickle of water around the edge of the pot after each handful of compost is all that is needed. Assuming that the compost is well drained, virtually every plant in active growth is given water when potted up rather than waiting several days for re-establishment. Opinions differ on the merits of this action. It is not, of course, appropriate with dormant plants or bulbs, which will only require extra watering when root growth resumes.

The compost level should be far enough below the pot rim to allow for topdressing. This is not merely cosmetic, but provides a barrier between the damper compost and the sometimes damp-sensitive foliage – secondary considerations include the mulching effect, the sterile, weed-free surfacing provided, and the support provided for the topgrowth whilst keeping the crown well aerated and reasonably dry.

It follows that a non-porous rock is generally preferable – some of the softer limestone chippings and tufa moss over very quickly, and their residual dampness can cause over-wintering difficulties. This is not to say that every pan needs to be topdressed with some form of rock: untreated bark or sphagnum moss are used with success for numerous woodland plants, or those that inhabit the high alpine moors. But the majority of alpine house plants are restricted to screes, vertical fissures and other habitats where surface drainage is efficient, and a layer of rock fragments or chippings, whilst not corresponding in exact detail to the genuine article, is a satisfactory substitute.

A really coarse, lime-free gravel is the most usual choice – builders' merchants can generally provide granite chippings and several grades of quartzite. The very fine grit sometimes sold as 'potting grit sand' is not advisable since it behaves as an aquifer – the reverse of what is intended. The 3mm chippings used in the body of the compost will do, but even larger material can be useful, especially for those plants that occupy rock crevices. Achieving the desired effect requires a degree of artistic licence, and the random appearance of shattered pieces of slate or schist (but be mindful that the latter may contain lime) is often more pleasing. Obtaining these may present difficulties: old slate roofing tiles are stocked by many builders' merchants, but are seldom more than a centimetre thick, although some firms will also provide 'undressed' slate (used for fireplace surrounds and the like) which can then be chipped off to suit. Collecting small quantities of rock on holiday is all very well, but a reasonably continuous layer of topdressing is envisaged, and if the few pieces have to be eked out as the plant occupies progressively larger pots, arranging them at intervals – a curious habit that still persists – then their practical purpose is lost, and it is very questionable whether the visual appeal is increased.

The depth of the topdressing will vary considerably, starting off with little more than a shallow covering with young seedlings, then between 2cm and 4cm when dealing with mature plants, and up to twice this depth with damp-sensitive bulbs such as *Iris nicolai* which have their basal plate in contact with the potting compost, but are encased in coarse chippings (graded for sale as 6mm and above). This latter system, whilst not foolproof, is a more certain way of coping with several of the more specialist southern hemisphere *Ranunculus* now seen in an increasing number of alpine houses (*RR. crithmifolius ssp paucifolius, haastii, semiverticillatus*) and the few summer dormant species of *Viola* from Northwest America (see Chapter 12) that make fitful appearances in cultivation.

5 Subsequent treatment

After repotting, a plant will require time to re-establish, and a period of several weeks can elapse before it becomes apparent whether or not the move has been successful. Certain genera have acquired a bad name for their supposed resentment of any attempt to disturb them (*Daphne* and *Dionysia* especially) and it is likely that this reputation has made matters worse, persuading their owners to put off the evil day until they become impossibly potbound. I find it

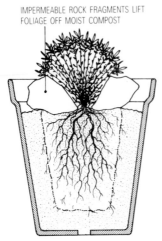

IMPERMEABLE ROCK FRAGMENTS LIFT
FOLIAGE OFF MOIST COMPOST

Figure 15   Topdressing

best to adopt a fatalistic attitude but follow the more obvious ground rules: never repot when the plant is in flower; remove soil from the rootball of older plants but avoid undue disturbance; choose the pot in keeping with the size of the root system rather than the top growth; make sure the fresh compost is filled in properly and *lightly* compressed rather than rammed against the roots; for preference repot whilst in active growth and aim to complete by early summer – exceptions could be cited, but do not balance the long list of failures.

The first action is to check the label and, if necessary, replace it. The date of the latest repot is recorded – some people prefer to store this information on a card index or, latterly, on disk. Depending on the time of year, the pot is either stood outside in a cool spot (a raised frame shaded from the south would be ideal) or placed back in the alpine house, though not in full sun. The roots may begin to refunction almost immediately, or it might take a while before the uptake of water con tinues as efficiently as before the operation, and if the foliage is exposed to warm sunshine then wilting will take place. Some plants are happiest if left on the floor of the alpine house, or on a second level of trays below the main benching, but this can lead to severe etiolation within a few days where young shoots are developing – the pulvinate species of *Phlox* and all but the woodland species of *Viola* show a marked resentment of this positioning.

As previously mentioned, unless the plant has purposely been potted when dormant, then it is watered when safely ensconced, standing the pot in a shallow soaktray for 5–10 minutes if overhead watering is likely to be resented. Unless the weather is very warm, it is unlikely to need a further watering until new growth is apparent, but this must be carefully checked, for even a temporary shortfall can hinder recovery.

The speed with which some plants adapt is surprising – seedlings especially often grow appreciably within the first week, and in early spring pans of campanulas push up new shoots with astonishing speed, doubtless triggered by the extra watering. Other plants are less compliant, and many sulk for a month, a season, or longer still. If a month has elapsed with no outward sign of improvement, the topsoil is scraped away and the crown/crowns checked for general vigour. The rootstock is then followed downwards, carefully excavating a small area to see (a) if the roots are growing into the new compost and (b) if there is any pathological evidence – loss of turgidity, change of colour, partial failure of root action. Performed in this way, the compost can be replaced and the pot replaced in its former position if all seems well.

In the minority of cases where inspection reveals something amiss, there is little alternative but to unpot, remove any damaged areas, spray with a fungicide (or soak in dilute systemic insecticide if pest damage is suspected) and repot in fresh compost. Waiting and hoping for the plant to rally of its own accord may well lead to disappointment.

It is said of a few plants, the 'vegetable sheep' species of *Raoulia* in particular, that a genuine difficulty exists in telling whether a specimen is alive or dead, and the cautionary tale of *R. eximia* receiving a show award long after life had departed continues to amuse. Those who have had the chance to compare the two states side by side will perhaps find this uncertainty puzzling. But should doubts remain, parting the central rosette with a pair of tweezers will reveal either tender new leaves or dry and shrivelled remnants. Note that the root system in itself is not an absolute guarantee – anyone who has grown Aretian androsaces will appreciate that a plant that has rotted through at the neck can still have a panful of live roots months after the plant has effectively died. With other genera, however, this can work to the gardener's advantage, and new rosettes of, for example, *Centaurea achtarovii* will often emerge following on from the demise of the original topgrowth.

Usually, though, a fortnight is long enough for the plant to have settled down. Some gardeners use a second coloured label to remind themselves of the degree of establishment – one colour for repotting carried out in the current year, another for plants that will need repotting when time allows.

9 The Covered Rock Garden

Not everyone will want to grow alpine plants in pots. There is a methodical tidiness about a well-maintained collection, but compared to say a scree bed or trough, the work involved in keeping the plants in good condition is appreciable. For example, there is a greater likelihood of them drying out, and the restricted root run makes it important to repot when the roots have become potbound. After a few months of use, the pots are likely to need scrubbing to bring them back to their original state of cleanliness, and whilst some alpines relish being replanted in fresh compost at regular intervals, others can be severely checked by the disturbance to their roots unless the operation is carried out very carefully. Beyond this, aesthetic judgements enter the argument – some people view the spectacle of the plant from the vast screes cramped into a terracotta pot with distaste, and even if they are not averse to the idea, lack of a local supplier may force on them a decision to try other methods of cultivation.

Several eminent gardeners and botanical institutions have given over glasshouse space to a rock garden protected from the local climate the year round. With some, the greenhouse plunge trays are deepened, then filled with a suitable compost, and the one-time pot plants inserted. Others have built the beds from ground level, usually digging out some of the compacted subsoil on which the alpine house was built and replacing it with an infill of potting compost or (a better plan) raising the bed up somewhat by using walling stone as a retaining wall. A third option is to provide a glass awning, cantilevered over the growing area or raised on corner supports, by which time we have started to leave the alpine house behind.

One occasionally sees the bed or tray merely filled with compost, levelled off and topdressed with pea gravel after planting. A more interesting appearance is assured if the surface is broken up with rockwork, providing the slight slopes, crevices and shaded rockfaces likely to be found in a bona fide alpine setting. If the garden is already raised off the ground, the weight of the added rock must necessarily be kept to a minimum. Tufa (sometimes referred to as travertine) is by far the most popular choice, being relatively light and with the additional advantage that it can be virtually cut to shape. Pieces left to stand outside for up to a year after having been quarried should be chosen. Even under glass the freshly cut surfaces will crumble and break away initially . . . and with few exceptions, only lime-loving plants can be used. The best solution is to devote one side of the alpine house to these plants, and make the opposite side lime-

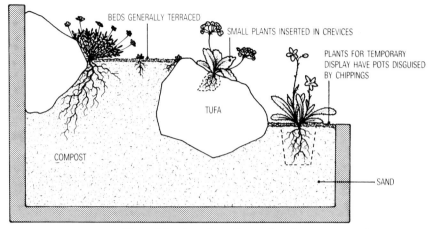

Figure 16   A rock garden under glass

free. Should larger pieces of slate that have not been split into thin fragments be obtainable, then these are perhaps the best choice, although the narrower pieces can be inserted on edge in clusters to provide a series of narrow crevices – a technique which requires an artistic eye if it is to look effective.

Beds built up directly from the ground are not hampered by the weight restriction, and several types of sandstone are favoured, providing an informal series of one or more terraces depending on the space available. As in any other rock garden, the effect of the rock placement has to be balanced against the consideration that general maintenance requires all areas to be readily access-ible, so the construction must be stable and provided with stones wide enough to stand upon at regular intervals. At Kew, where the alpine house is furnished with Sussex sandstone on a grand scale, those who look after the collection are able to step from level to level and attend to plants growing well beyond arm's reach. The amateur equivalents, unlikely to be more than 2m from front to back, do not pose quite the same problem, and it is unlikely that the vertical scale will be very pronounced. Once the general level has been decided upon, an effective means of providing further elevation is to cement a continuous line of concrete slabs along the back, buried for up to a third of their height for stability, and build against this. With a free standing alpine house, the effect from the outside is not overly attractive, however, and a less ambitious construction, giving the effect of several outcrops distributed along the bed, involves the use of far fewer stones.

The major chore involved is mixing compost, which should correspond to that used for growing alpines in pots (see Chapter 8). A well-drained mix, neutral in reaction, such as two part John Innes No. 2 and one of sharp grit will suit the needs of many plants, although after the first few years, supplementary feeding is likely to be necessary. An unresolved problem is that of soluble salts, principally nitrates, gradually building up, and it is important that water should be able to drain away easily, either by the provision of drainage holes in trays supported on benching, or by making sure that the subsoil is not over-compacted if beds are constructed at ground level. The depth of compost should not be less than 15cm, and where possible 20–30cm.

It remains unclear exactly how long such beds will endure before 'soil sickness' or some other nebulous ailment persuades the owner to clear out the contents and start again, but several European examples started off in the 1950s and 1960s are still in use, and as the approach has gained in popularity, more information on this aspect can be expected to filter through. What has to be accepted is that a degree of replanting is inevitable – as in the open rock garden some plants will do surprisingly well and soon outgrow their allotted space, whereas others will require experimental plantings in several areas, and even then may not find conditions to their liking.

Watering can be administered by perforated underground tubing which floods the lower growing medium, or in some instances by spray lines and mist units which soak the plants from above, but neither is likely to prove completely satisfactory, being too random to satisfy the diverse needs of the plants grown. Spot watering by hand allows summer-dormant, tuberous-rooted plants to be grown in the same general area as others which will tolerate overhead watering, and downy cushions that appreciate a moist compost when in growth, but may not relish water lodging in their foliage. Where doubts exist over whether enough water is reaching the root system, the best plan is to scrape away the topdressing (lifting up the spreading mat of foliage where required) and apply water to the exposed compost as necessary, giving time for it to soak in and reapplying before returning the barrier layer of chippings which inhibits dampness around the crown.

A number of alpine houses open to the public reserve areas where the plants on display come from a back-up of pot-grown specimens, buried in plunge material which is disguised by the surface dressing to given an impression of the plants having permanent residence there. The plants are exchanged for others that differ in their time of flowering to provide continued interest almost the year round. Very seldom is this system utilised in private gardens.

Planting alpines directly into the ground can be beneficial to both the appearance and the health of many species that are never quite satisfactory when grown in pots. It may be they look untidy because of their loose growth which takes on a quite different appearance if allowed to cascade down a rock face – *Asperula suberosa* is immeasurably improved in this way, and so too are the pretty, summer flowering chasmophytic hypericums such as *H. ericoides* and *H. pallens*. Others mould their annual flowering stems to the contours of the rock, and can be a nuisance if these snake out and cover the top of neighbouring pots: *Campanula rupestris* comes into this category. It has the added burden of being (normally) short lived, but will seed into crevices if planted out, as too will the glaucous, frilly tufts of *Sarcocapnos enneaphylla*, which do not take well to repotting, their foliage being brittle and their roots easily damaged. Then again, some plants will grow equally well in pots or planted out, but are highly ornamental over a long period and are worthy of inclusion for this feature alone. Ferns of the genus *Cheilanthes* are now represented from across the whole range of their distribution, and repeat blooming plants such as *Erodium corsicum* also qualify.

Some plants do not readily form a central stand of growth, and if kept in a pot their shoots come up in a ring at the edge with a disconcerting gap in the middle. It is generally found that the tuberous-rooted *Corydalis* (specifically the central Asian species of section Leonticoides such as *C. popovii*) suffer from this drawback, and it is also noticeable in several species of *Cyclamen* where the flower stem does not rise more or less vertically from the tuber – *C. trochopter-anthum*, for example. Dodges such as planting the pot inside a large one and then topdressing as a disguise only partially overcome this tendency, and only in skilled hands do the results bear any comparison with corms grown in the open border. The random appearance of the shoots is one of the delights of this form of gardening: in a pot the contents are precisely identified, whereas in the open border plants can be left to seed around (or more accurately, the better mannered can) and form continuous drifts, or send their shoots here and there, shifting territory from year to year.

Alpines that spread beyond the standard pot size need not be planted outside (where their size prevents adequate covering against winter wet), though they can be pruned if they over extend their territory. Often they will tolerate outdoor life in some areas and in some seasons – *Verbascum* 'Letitia' and *Salvia caespitosa* are typical examples, but may take exception to some climatic combinations and die within a few weeks. Or they may require carefully controlled watering at all times of the year, yet form a root system that is difficult to contain within a pot. The beautiful clear yellow *Iris barnumae* ssp. *barnumae* forma *urmiensis*, thankfully more difficult to enunciate than it is to grow, is one of a number of Oncocyclus Iris that pose this problem, and if given a good depth of well-drained compost, regularly 'fed' and the dormant rhizomes split every three years or so, proves an ideal plant for a position in full sun.

Pests of various descriptions find the rockwork equally congenial, and ants in particular may choose to build their nests in the dry crevices, for which reason some gardeners add an insecticide to the compost at planting time. Birds too may fly in and peck at the mats of foliage with disastrous results, and to prevent this it is necessary either to drape a length of netting across the doorway, or perhaps construct a wire frame to block their interest.

10 Propagation

The limited availability of some alpine house plants and the constant search for means of increasing their stocks makes it essential for the gardener to learn how to propagate them. A tendency to rely on others has led to many good plants falling out of general cultivation – everyone assumes that someone else must be doing the job, and by the time the assumption is challenged, the species in question has all but disappeared. Conversely, for most of us it is a means to an end, and overcommitting oneself by sowing hundreds of seed pots, taking cuttings whenever a half ripe shoot appears, and nurturing row after row of divisions, leaves little time or space to bring the products of this hard work to healthy maturity. So there has to be a balance. Usually the activity is forced upon us at an early stage. We discuss a plant with an acquaintance, and weeks later a packet of seeds arrives through the post. Or we visit a garden where the owner breaks a few shoots off some shrub admired in passing, pokes them in a polythene bag and sends us on our way. If we are lucky enough to live where a nurseryman can be contacted in person or through a catalogue, then a proportion of alpine plants can be grown on from a stage that has only called upon our ability to write a cheque, but few would deny the satisfaction of being responsible for a plant from its first root and shoot.

Owning just one specimen of a particular plant is always a risk – make one serious mistake and it could be killed. Moreover, the need to experiment is thwarted: tried and tested methods have to be used, for fear that a radical departure might cause irreversible damage. Luckily, there are comparatively few alpines that spurn our attempts to propagate them, and although a number have their foibles, the basic techniques used are really quite simple.

Results will vary depending on the quality of the material, the skill of the would-be cultivator in handling it and the environment provided, but it is worth remembering that a battery of expensive equipment is not necessary, and that though there may be an optimum time to carry out some of the procedures mentioned, the process is a year-round one. Several plants owe their presence in our gardens to an alert owner who managed to salvage propagating material from an ailing plant, and the timing of the operation did not necessarily coincide with that recommended by the gardening manuals.

The various methods of vegetative propagation are an excellent means of multiplying the plants we already grow, but raising from seed is by far the most significant means of introducing new material, and offers the opportunity to select and diversify rather than simply duplicate.

74

Raising plants from seed _____

Anyone handling seed soon comes to realise that it is as highly and variously adapted to its environment as the plants themselves. Our efforts to persuade it to germinate must take account of this, stopping short, however, of the now discredited rituals of heaping snow on the sown pots, or freezing them solid before putting them against a radiator.

The first fallacy to dismiss is that seed is somehow inert – even when dry (i.e. only 5–10 per cent of the total weight comprising water) the normal cell structures are visible through a microscope, and although the seed coat provides protection, damage can occur through incorrect storing or climatic extremes, quite apart from the spontaneous fall-off in viability that occurs as the seed ages. Stored dry in silica gel at a constant temperature of around freezing point, the process of ageing can be significantly slowed down, but too often seed is kept under inadequate conditions, which either force a deeper dormancy or lead to its death. In general, seeds exposed to ordinary atmospheric humidity will tend to lose their viability.

Factors affecting germination
Recognising good seed is not always straightforward, but assuming that all is well in this respect, uneven or poor germination can be attributed to a number of factors:

(1) Sowing too deeply. The smaller the seed, the less covering it is likely to need, so that with any seed it is not possible to handle individually, sprinkling the batch on top of the seedpan and soaking it from below until the surface appears moist will be quite adequate. Otherwise, if germination does take place, a small embryo may not have the reserves to enable the shoot to extend to the soil surface, and there is evidence of gaseous germination inhibitors that take effect with increasing depth. Covering to the depth of the seeds diameter is usually adequate.

(2) Insufficient light. This point is complementary with the above, and is presumably a mechanism to protect seed from germinating too deeply. Gardeners will be familiar with the way in which a recently turned piece of ground acquires a covering of weed seedlings where the dormant seed has been brought to the surface. A few genera are known to respond to darkness, and it is suggested that this is linked to the absence of chlorophyll in the capsule or bracts housing the seed as it matures. However, even plants said to germinate better if light is excluded – *Phlox*, for example – seem to come up just as well when exposed to normal lighting, and covering the pots with a light screen is seldom necessary.

(3) Stratification. This is the process whereby seed, already moistened so that the embryos have begun to take up water, is exposed to low temperatures,

which has a cumulative effect until the minimum chilling requirement for the particular species is satisfied. For most gardeners, a 'normal' winter will do the trick, and a temperature of between freezing point and 5°C is perfectly adequate. This helps to prevent the seedlings from appearing too early and being destroyed, especially since a diurnal fluctuation between warm days and cold nights corresponding to spring conditions can trigger shoot emergence. The length of exposure can extend from one to six months, but a consistent minimum is not essential, although some gardeners place their pots in the salad drawer of a domestic refrigerator once the seed is imbibed, which can be adjusted to an appropriate setting.

(4) Lack of water. Once the seed is sown, the aim is to keep the compost moist, whether the time lapse is a matter of weeks or years. If the seed coat is toughened, the shoot may have difficulty in emerging, and even if the radicle appears and shoot growth begins, the seed coat is not always shed (*Nototriche* seedlings often have this difficulty) and its mechanical removal with forceps or nail scissors usually damages the trapped cotyledons.

The seed frequently has a water-soluble germination inhibitor, and this has to be leached out before growth can take place. This explains why it can help to soak old seed, placing it in a shallow depth of cold water (with a few plants from very dry, hot areas, boiling water is used instead) for a period of 24 hours, replacing the water half way through the period. With very fine seed, of course, this separate treatment is impossible, and where any dryness can be fatal (most Ericaceae) it is better to surface sow onto milled sphagnum, placing the pots under a propagator shield or translucent covering where humidity can be maintained.

After the initial and rapid uptake of water, when it is possible to see that the 'plumped up' seed has increased its weight and in effect revived, there is commonly a delay, during which time a variety of metabolic processes are initiated, before further absorption is accompanied by the visible signs of germination. Allowing the compost to dry out before this second phase is completed accounts for a proportion of the failed seed pans that even the most successful gardeners experience.

(5) An adaptation in areas where the climate can be erratic is the staggered germination of seed, so that seedlings can be expected over a period of five years and frequently much longer. The seed may even be dimorphic – as in certain members of the Compositae, where the smaller seeds have an inbuilt dormancy enabling them to act as a reserve in the soil. They may then spring to life years later when an adverse climatic sequence has killed the plants that developed earlier from the larger, disc seeds at the centre of the flowerhead. This phased germination is also familiar to those who have sown seed of *Ranunculus*, *Viola* or *Fritillaria* (the seeds that originate at the apex of the capsule awakening last) and numerous others.

(6) The seed coat, as observed earlier, helps to protect against moisture loss,

but can act as a barrier that needs to be breached before germination can proceed. Rather than carry this out as a matter of course, I prefer to reserve abrading treatments for seed that has not shown any progress two seasons after sowing. This way, seed of *Astragalus* (and numerous other Leguminosae) will frequently sprout without the risk of removing the seed coat too vigorously and damaging the embryo, as can happen when rubbing sandpaper against it or nicking the tip with a sharp knife.

Sowing

Having looked at the major reasons for non germination, we can now rehearse the procedure for sowing the seed and maintaining the seedlings in their early stages.

For preference, a proportion of the seed should be sown immediately it is received. Some genera–*Salix* is a notorious example – have a viability span of less than a month, and several others (notably the Petiolarid section of *Primula* and *Corydalis*) do very much better if transferred to a seedpan as soon as the capsules gape open, although a reduced spasmodic germination can be expected even from dried seed. There is evidence to support the view that seed of many high alpines has no intrinsic dormancy mechanism, but that temperatures/moisture levels are too low, or ripening takes place too late in the season, for germination to come about before the snow melts in the following spring. Seed brought back by expeditions to regions where such plants occur can sometimes awaken within days of a summer sowing (Cruciferae, Compositae and Caryophyllaceae among others show this tendency) and since the young plants may not develop sufficiently to withstand a harsh lowland winter, it is best to retain half the seed and sow this after the turn of the year, keeping the packet in aluminum foil meanwhile, placed in a cool, dry place. Against this, seed of *Gentiana*, whether European, Himalayan or Andean, has not germinated for me until it has passed through a winter, and there are doubtless numerous other exceptions to the list of high alpines that have the potential to sprout soon after they are shed.

The seed compost can usually be standardised, the principal requirements being that it should be open in texture, moisture retentive and not over-rich. Using a commercially prepared formula (John Innes No. 1) for the 'soil' part of the compost does away with the need for sterilisation of the medium, and mixed with an equal bulk of lime-free grit will satisfy most of the plants likely to be grown. The small amount of lime contained in the former is unlikely to harm even plants that are restricted to acid soils. However, such plants frequently grow in a humus-rich medium, and so the compost can be modified by adding to these ingredients an equal part of sphagnum moss peat. Warnings that John Innes compost over ten weeks old should not be used are baffling, since it is likely to remain in the seed pan for a minimum of three months, and does not seem to have had a harmful effect over much longer periods. Some people prefer to use a peat-based compost, dispensing with the loam element altogether but, as with the mature plants, this is not critical. More important is that the ingredients should be relatively free from pathogens, easily and cheaply available, and consistent in quality.

Plants requiring a constantly moist root run and high humidity are treated slightly differently. Sphagnum moss is dried and chopped up with a pair of kitchen scissors, resoaking it before sowing the seed and placing the pots in an unheated propagator. A slow release fertiliser is sometimes added, but the plants frequently have minimal nutritional needs and survive quite happily in the original compost until their growth makes pricking out necessary.

To conserve space and allow for easy replacement as signs of germination appear, one size of pot is used (7.5cm), and whereas the mature plants are predominantly housed in terracotta plantpots, in the early stages plastic ones are satisfactory. These do not dry out as easily as their clay counterparts, and plant roots do not cling to their inner surface in the annoying way that they can with the alternative. Except for the largest of seeds – *Paeonia*, for instance – this size allows for an adequate number of seedlings, but commercially (and for the rare occasions when a large quantity of plants may be required) larger pots and even the plastic seed trays more familiar to those who raise bedding annuals are useful. Supposedly difficult plants like *Campanula morettiana*, *Paraquilegia anemonoides* and *Soldanella minima* have been grown by the hundreds using this method, pricking them out at an early stage into evenly spaced rows of up to 50 young plants in identical trays, before potting off singly when the roots appear through the drainage holes.

With plants that suffer a check in growth when the root is disturbed, but have seeds large enough for space sowing, it is worth putting them two in a pot and discarding the weaker seedling should both germinate. This does away with the possibility of disentangling one root system from a mass of others, but is only worth trying with 'special' plants where germination percentages are high enough to justify the extra space taken up. Once a root system has built up in the original pot, it can usually be moved to a larger size without significant damage. Sweet pea growers employ a similar trick, and the related *Astragalus* can benefit from such treatment – *Daphne*, *Lupinus* and *Sarcocapnos* are others that come to mind.

Before the seed is sown, a label should be made out with the name of the plant, source, date of sowing and (occasionally) number of seeds all logged on it. Some people prefer to use a reference number alone, which can be checked back to a stockbook where there is more space to record the full details. The plastic labels widely available turn brittle through the action of sunlight and many annotations in waterproof ink do not last long after the first year, but pencil markings can remain legible for rather longer, especially if the label is pushed down so that only the top few centimetres are exposed. This also lessens the risk of snapping it off whilst moving neighbouring pots.

The seed pots are filled with a centimetre of washed grit, which prevents the compost falling through the drainage holes (these vary greatly from one manufacturer to another) and at potting on time means that the root ends can be freed easily of any material that might hold them in a tangle. On top of this goes the compost, settled by tapping the base of the pot on a hard surface so that it comes at least one centimentre below the rim. It will sink further when moistened, but this allows room for a topdressing of grit, which should be washed before use – it is often full of silt when purchased, and this can lead to a capping which encourages moss growth.

Normally a number of different seed packets will have been involved, and unless care is exercised at this stage, it is quite possible to mix up the labels. To avoid this, the labels should be written and placed immediately in the requisite number of pots, which are kept well away from the potting bench, fetching each in turn and matching it up against the seed packet before sowing. This also prevents stray seedlings from appearing in the wrong pots, as sometimes happens when handling a mixed batch.

Where practicable, the seeds are sown between 5mm and 15mm apart, depending on their size, but very fine seed is emptied into the clean, dry palm of one hand and deftly sprinkled with the thumb and forefinger of the other. Mixing with dry sand to achieve an even distribution has always seemed to me a waste of time and results have been no better – indeed on the whole worse. As mentioned earlier, sowing too deeply is a frequent cause of failure, but with larger seed a *light* scattering of compost topped off with 3mm grit is suitable. The surface on which the seed is sown should be even but not compacted.

To complete, the pots are soaked from below until the surface grit shows signs of dampness. At this point some growers prefer to leave them outside until germination is visible, but they are safer in either a covered seed frame or on trays underneath the alpine house benching, provided that light reaches this area. Otherwise heavy rain and winds can displace the surface dressing and the seeds lying only just beneath, whilst predators cull the newly emerging seedlings before they can be rescued. Earthworms can be a nuisance even in a cold frame, entering through the drainage holes and churning the contents of the pot, leaving soil casts on the surface as well.

When the seedlings appear

How often the seed pots should be checked depends on the time of year and the position chosen. Until the first burst of spring weather triggers off widespread emergence, once a week is probably sufficient, making sure that the compost is still moist across the whole batch in the process. The first appearance of a cotyledon is the sign to move the pot to a cool but well-lit part of the alpine house. In practice, this means that from late winter onwards a tray just inside the alpine house door is left free to fill up gradually with newly emerged seedlings. Those that appear later in the year will need light shading and the risk of them drying out will increase.

Opinion is divided upon how soon to prick out the seedlings, but my own preference is to do so at a relatively early stage if time allows, except when handling bulbous or summer dormant plants, which are left until their second dormancy, unless badly overcrowded, before the dry soil is knocked out and the small plants installed in more spacious quarters. With the general run of alpines, though, moving the tiny seedlings early on helps to prevent the roots entwining below ground or the topgrowth developing to a stage where, when disturbance occurs, it places a heavy demand on the damaged root system.

As soon as the first true leaf appears, therefore, and on occasion even before, the label is removed, the pot knocked sharply on its side and – with luck – the still intact rootball cradled in the hand or eased onto a mound of potting compost, ensuring all the while that the foliage is not crushed. Certainly the pot should not have been recently watered, but nor should its contents have dried out: the ideal to aim at is barely moist to the touch, and progress towards this end can be checked by removing a portion of the topdressing beforehand.

The amount of root made by the plants can surprise all but the most seasoned gardeners. Gently prodding the compost with a dibber or the end of a pencil will separate the different root systems, and again by this stage a suitable potting compost should have been prepared, and clean pots made ready to receive the young plants. The less time the plants are out of the soil the better. If there are plenty to choose from, the weak-looking seedlings are thrown away unless they appear to differ from the rest in some other respect. Growing on the whole batch can lead to unexpected variation in the most unpromising individuals, but the space and time required are limiting factors. Suppose that just ten pots (a modest total) germinate and produce 20 seedlings apiece . . . that means a total of an extra 200 plants to find room for, quite apart from the added space needed for plants that have been repotted and other sources of new material.

Picking the seedling up by the tip of the cotyledon, it is held at roughly the right level over a 3.5cm diameter pot (the smaller 'thumb' pots are still seen in both clay and plastic versions, and can be useful for really tiny seedlings such as some ourisias, gentians, jasiones etc.) and compost is trickled around the root, which if branched is encouraged to spread by separating it with the pointed end of the dibber and filling the gap with further compost. Except for highly damp-intolerant plants, a carefully applied trickle of water when the pot is half full and again round the edge when the desired level has been reached provides a firming, after which the plant is kept shaded for a minimum of 48 hours to recuperate. A liquid application of copper fungicide is sometimes used at this stage to discourage damping off diseases, but providing the plant tissues have not been badly bruised and the compost has been sterilised, this is not really necessary.

Where the plant is known to be difficult to cultivate, several different treatments can be tried, and the details recorded against the original entry in the stock book. For instance, just a proportion of the batch might be sprayed with a fungicide, some might be potted in a peat-based, others in loam-based compost, the natural time of pricking out might be delayed for a portion of the crop and so on.

An alternative is to thin out the original seedlings, leaving just a few well distributed around the pot. This is wasteful of material and although the plants may develop well in the uncrowded area, they seldom surge away with the enthusiasm that newly repotted seedlings repeatedly do, doubling in size within a few weeks.

One bonus the alpine house gardener is entitled to expect is the appearance of chance seedlings – often in the most unlikely spots. In fact they can be a nuisance if they appear in a well-established neighbouring pan and are not removed before their roots go down to mingle with those of the rightful occupant. Emerging from the plunge they are less of a problem, and can easily be removed with the roots intact and potted up if required. Because a wide range of species are brought into contact, chance hybrids and bigeneric crosses have come about in this way. *Verbascum* 'Letitia', a widely grown plant that survives all but the wettest winters in the open, appeared at Wisley from a liaison between *V. spinosum* and *V. dumulosum* (neither of which can be trusted outside without reservation) and of the several *Dionysia* hybrids that have spread from Göteborg Botanic Garden, the one between *D. aretioides* and *D. teucrioides* shows signs of being a valuable addition to the range. The numerous hybrids that involve *Primula allionii* in their parentage have some-times come about accidentally, and curiosity plants like *Campanula piperi* × *cenisia* and the invaluable *Campanula* 'Joe Elliott' show that it is advisable to look carefully before weeding.

Topgrowth cuttings

It isn't always possible to persuade a plant to set viable seed in cultivation – how often does one see seed setting on classic alpine house plants like *Linum aretioides*, *Viola delphinantha* or *Raoulia mammillaris* away from their native homes? In other instances, where cross fertilisation is required, the absence of a suitable partner can prevent the process. Moreover, alpine gardeners tend to select and favour particular clones, and vegetative propagation is the only means of maintaining them. The numerous hybrids that are grown, even if they are not sterile, will not produce seedlings whose worth can be guaranteed in advance. And since alpine house specimens frequently need trimming into shape, the growth removed should be put to use where possible on a waste not, want not basis.

As more is learned about the likely behaviour of alpine plants in cultivation, the notion that cuttings are taken only in high summer becomes progressively less relevant. We now realise that with rare material particularly, it is worth attempting propagation at any time of the year if the plant shows signs of distress. Supplementary lighting and the advent of easily usable heated propagating units have aided our attempts to root cuttings off season, and for the less sophisticated the simple expedient of taking a potful into the dwelling house can be successful.

Maintenance and materials
Because the detached shoots are without roots, but have leaves that continue to lose water reserves, the alpine house owner must provide conditions that

prevent undue transpiration and keep the exposed portion of the cutting cool, yet allow in enough sunlight not to inhibit photosynthesis. Rewetting the rooting medium can lead to conditions that favour plant diseases, but not all alpines can tolerate the high humidity of growing under the perspex hood of a propagator.

For these, a partially shaded frame is ideal, although successful results have been had by rooting them on the open alpine house bench in the sand plunge. It is important to choose a position where the sun cannot strike directly, because if the top layer of sand dries out before any roots have formed, obviously the cuttings will perish. This is an argument in favour of attempting to root material earlier in the year. Another way round the problem is to install a mist propagation bench – an overhead system of nozzles that produce a fine spray of water whenever a sensor detects that the film of water that covers the foliage has evaporated. Such misting systems affects the overall environment of the alpine house, the high humidity they guarantee being difficult to confine to the immediate area of the cutting bench. For this reason they are best located in a separate unit. Moreover, a number of the cuttings placed on an open bench to lessen the problem of damping off would resent water being sprayed on their foliage.

The subdued light of the floor area under the benching can be utilised for such plants, but it is necessary to avoid any areas where shade cast by surrounding structures outside (cold frames, raised beds, etc.) prevents light from ever penetrating. As an aside, it is noticeable that if a plant is placed here for a few days prior to taking cutting material, the etiolated growths that develop root more easily. Nurserymen keep stock plants explicitly for the purpose of propagating batches of material from them, not worrying greatly about the unkempt appearance of the clipped-over source; one would hesitate before treating a specimen plant in this fashion, but many woody species that do not root easily otherwise respond well if cuttings are prepared from the drawn growth.

While cuttings of easily grown alpines can usually be rooted outside in pots left in a shaded position, with more unusual or demanding plants it is generally best to root them under glass. And because they root at different rates it is preferable to separate them by placing each species in a different pot, which can be moved when rooting occurs without disturbing others that take longer to do so. Older gardeners may still favour clay pots, but the high humidity means that they can quickly become covered in algae, and are less easy to sterilise than their plastic counterparts.

The usual arrangement is to utilise a seed tray. Those without drainage holes are probably better, because once a plastic propagator hood has been fitted invertebrate pests cannot gain access, and since repeated watering will not be necessary, there is no need to syphon away excess water. A standard 27cm × 44cm model will accommodate ten 7.5cm pots – and if square pots are chosen, half as many again. At the same time, the aim should be not to crowd the area, just as for preference the foliage of the separate cuttings should not be touching. Quite apart from the difficulties of levering out a rooted plant from amongst a mass of immature material, any of the prepared shoots that fail may become infected with fungal spores, and disease transmission is rapid in overcrowded conditions.

Unless it is intended to let the rooted cuttings establish before attempting to transplant them, there is no need to devise a 'compost' as such. The aeration and water-holding capacity of several aggregates, notably vermiculite and perlite, have led to their widespread use as rooting media, but for the tiny cuttings, perhaps just a few millimetres long, that some alpine plants provide, it is difficult to bed the small shoot in so that firm contact is achieved.

Excellent results can be achieved using only non-calcareous silver sand or, where extra moisture retention is thought desirable, equal parts of this and peat which has been broken down so that any coarse strands or fibres are removed. I am dubious about the standard advice to use the coarsest sand available – anything sold as 'gritsand' for example is likely to have particles varying in size up to a centimentre. Given that the sand has a granular texture and drains fairly freely, some latitude can be allowed, and whereas it is customary to use a coarse grade of what is generally labelled 'horticultural silver sand' where the grist is from 3mm downwards, much finer mixtures, their visual texture similar to demerara sugar, are every bit as good.

Some people strain the sand through muslin to rid it of any impurities, before pouring boiling water through it to provide the cuttings with a clean start. In practice, if bought ready bagged this first washing is often superfluous. For the small amount needed at any one time by the majority of amateur gardeners, it is more practical to fill the required number of pots with sand, pour boiling water from the spout of a kettle into the centre of each, and leave to cool. If the bottom layer of the pot is filled with a mixture of peat and sand, this prevents the sand from pouring out of the drainage holes when the operation takes place. Before the cuttings are inserted, a watering of benomyl (diluted at half strength) is a further refinement.

Method and timing

Now for the cutting itself. Normally single shoots are chosen – the exception being those tightly imbricated plants whose individual rosettes are minute, where tracing a cluster down to the main 'branch' is preferable. Another point here: the cuttings are normally derived from the outer area of the plant, where the most recent growth is located – at least with cushion-forming species. With more shrubby material, the choice of site for removal is wider, and all things being equal, it provides a chance to remove any aberrant growths. The size of the cutting will vary enormously – an average of 20 – 40mm can be expected, but with minutely rosetted plants such as *Saxifraga squarrosa* and the smaller species of *Dionysia*, a length of approximately 5mm is more likely.

It is advantageous if material can be rooted early enough in the year for subsequent growth to take place, since very young plantlets do not always have the reserves to see them through the winter. The exception to this rule is for hardwood cuttings, i.e. those that do not form annual deciduous shoots but set resting buds, which can be seen developing soon after the post-flowering extension growth has developed. These are taken from late summer onwards, and will usually root when the source plant comes into leaf the following spring. Some will probably produce a few roots the same autumn, but it is better not to disturb them before the winter is over. Several of the relatively small numbers of ericaceous plants that do well under alpine house conditions can be propagated in this way – notably the dwarf forms of *Menziesia ciliicalyx*, the floriferous hybrids between *Rhodothamnus chamaecistus* and *Kalmiopsis leachiana* and the early flowering *Arcterica nana*.

Normally though, cuttings are taken when the plants are in active growth, avoiding the blooming period since at this time every shoot may terminate in a flower. The most popular time to attempt this form of propagation is in the wake of flowering, either from the soft new growth or at various stages as the shoots become firmer and are said to 'ripen'. Many will root with ease at almost any stage: others seem more selective, and only one batch will be successful. No exact dates can be given, since the development of the shoot progresses at a different rate from year to year. To illustrate, I had consistent success with *Linum elegans* by taking standard tip cuttings in mid-June, some three weeks to a month after flowering was completed. Two successive mild winters led to an earlier display, and the first time adhering to the 'traditional' date led to complete failure, whereas after the second the cuttings were selected a fortnight earlier, which brought a return to satisfactory results.

High temperatures can inhibit rooting, not just because the risk of the rooting medium drying out increases, but probably because in plants from regions that experience hot dry summers, growth is confined to the autumn and more especially the early spring. Plants like *Convolvulus boissieri* (Plate 13), the woolly leaved Turkish veronicas (*V. bombycina*, *V. caespitosa*, *V. thymoides*) and similarly clad members of the genus *Eriogonum* will root within a matter of a few weeks if inserted in late spring, whereas those batches from later on have seldom been potted before mid-autumn. The same is true of *Dionysia*, which like the foregoing are best placed in damp sand and positioned out of direct sunlight.

The optimum temperature of the rooting medium for root growth lies within the range of 15–24°C, which helps to explain why results are not always improved by a hot summer, whereas in a cool one root formation will merely tend to be delayed.

Short growth spurs coming off firm wood are generally taken with a heel – the shoot is held towards the base and pulled downwards and towards the handler. This is most successful when the growth is still flexible, trimming away the short fluke only as far as the firm base. Roots will usually form from this surface, unlike other cuttings where they usually emanate from a node.

It is not usually necessary to pinch out the tip of the cutting or reduce the area of the leaves after trimming, and although the advice to leave fleshy cuttings to dry off before inserting them is still occasionally heard, it remains sound practice to take only a few at a time and place them into their rooting medium as quickly as possible. However, if kept wrapped in damp tissue paper or even a closed polythene bag, material of some alpines can be kept in good condition for several days. Plants of the seldom-cultivated *Oxalis microphylla* have been raised in this way, transporting a couple of the radial branches from their home high in the Argentinian Andes, stripping off the dense covering of marcescent leaves on returning several days later, and placing them in pure sand, having sectioned off the shoot 3cm from its apex.

The actual cut needs to be made cleanly. The smaller sizes of pruning knives are adequate if kept sharp and sterilised between using on one batch of a species and transferring to another. Cross contamination, particularly with virus diseases, is almost inevitable if this precaution is neglected. Better still is the judicious use of a razor blade or the longhandled scissors used to reduce the number of fruits on a bunch of grapes or for delicate surgical work. The latter enable the excision of material whilst allowing the gardener to obtain a clear view of where the cut should be made, and without breaking off brittle growth in the immediate area.

With the smallest cuttings, it is difficult to obtain a sufficient length of stem (the caudicle) to allow for satisfactory insertion in the growing medium. But with a normal leafy shoot, the normal practice is simply to strip away the lower leaves, and push the exposed stem in the sand, burying the first node or, with plants that send up subsoil shoots (*Phlox*, some species of *Viola* etc.), at least two. Where the leaves are widely spaced, an accurate cut can be made just below a leaf joint, but where the stem is obscured by old leaves or dense growth, the method is to cut to the approximate length required, expose the stem and set firmly in the pot.

Any foliage that is buried under the surface will tend to rot – the same goes for snags of the discarded leaf bases – and where they cannot be readily peeled away, some people prefer to cut them off with a razor blade. This is not always possible, and it is awkward not to break off the stem when dealing with thin or otherwise fragile shoots.

Several products, normally based on indol-butyric acid, are available under the banner of rooting hormone solutions, and whilst their use is optional, it is worth experimenting if untreated cuttings do not yield good results. They may contain a fungicide, and this helps with easily rotting species. Manufacturers may recommend that those preparations diluted with water are applied at different concentrations depending on the plant chosen and the time of year. I have seen several species of *Daphne* (*D. cneorum*, *D. pygmaea*, *D. jasminea* and *D. petraea*) where treatment appears to have aided or speeded up rooting, and have myself rooted *Linum aretioides* and *Erinacea anthyllis* this way, when normal attempts have all failed.

If the cutting has a firm base, it may be possible to push it easily into the moistened sand/rooting mix, but the usual practice is to make a small hole with the point of a clean plant label, drop the shoot in to level where the leaves remain, and then firm by applying pressure with a fingertip from either side.

With a round pot, it is easiest to place the first in the centre and work outwards – if a whole trayful are needed, then they can be straightforwardly lined out. Enough space should be left to enable a thin stream of water to be poured between each one which helps further to firm them, but this is not always necessary. Whether they are watered overhead depends on the cuttings chosen and the time of year – if the leaves are hairy, 'silver', woolly or felt-like then certainly not.

Establishment

Rooting can take place surprisingly quickly: *Viola alpina* has been ready for potting up within a fortnight when taken in mid-spring, but my personal record is still held by *Campanula* 'Joe Elliott' which took under a week to root from a basal shoot pulled off the old network of crowns in mid March and placed in full sun during a warm spell. For the period mid-spring – early autumn a weekly inspection is adequate, both to check for signs of rooting and the possibility of dead shoots which, unless removed straight away, can soon contaminate the whole batch.

Recognising when a propagule has begun to root is not quite as straight-forward as is sometimes suggested. Renewed growth is the *usual* confirmation, but some plants are quite capable of doing this before initiating root growth. The only resolve is to take the blade of a small knife or the narrow end of a dibber, prod it into the sand a few centimetres away and prise upwards, very carefully supporting the cutting with the thumb and forefinger of the other hand.

If the result is negative, it must be bedded in again firmly, because unless the cutting is in close contact with the sand, it is very likely to wilt. Some plants assist here by having a wiry stolon that can be anchored in with the base of the rosette rotting on the surface. Some of the beautiful Himalayan androsaces show this feature and although considered a challenge to grow on, plants like *Androsace robusta* forma *breviscapa* will in fact root very easily if the tiny rings of new rosettes that rise up as the flowers fade are left a few weeks to develop, and then in late spring or early summer cut off with a few centimetres of their 'spoke' left on.

Assuming that roots have formed, plants known to be resentful of disturb-ance are best moved at an early stage, not into the compost that will be utilised for the plant at maturity, but into one containing a proportion of sand, or where a central plug of sand lessens the shock of displacement. A small pot is used and the young plant generally watered in (briefly dipping the pot up to half way in a soak tray if it needs summer glass protection) then given a chance to establish by screening it from strong sunlight for a few days. When the topgrowth begins to develop, or roots appear through the drainage holes, the hardest part is usually past. Just as pricking out accounts for a high percentage of losses among seedlings, moving freshly rooted cuttings is a testing time requiring equal attention.

10. The easily-grown *Eranthis* 'Guinea Gold' provides early colour in the alpine house.

11. *Cyclamen repandum*

12. One of several hybrids (*Clematis marmoraria* × *petriei*) now widely grown

13. *Convolvulus bossieri*, grown in a pot plunged in sand

14. *Daphne cneorum* var. *pygmaea*, seldom as compact in cultivation as in the wild

Other forms of propagation

There are various other ways of increasing stocks of alpine house plants, one of which, micropropagation, may well become of increasing significance to the amateur gardener. The others are useful but of lesser importance.

Division

For plants that multiply their crowns, producing basal growths that subdivide until an interlocking series of plants is achieved with a multiple root system, splitting the clumps every few years can be a way of rejuvenating them as well as providing new stock. Much the same is true of bulbous plants, notably species of *Crocus* and *Narcissus*, that if left will tend to become overcongested until bulbs begin to appear at the surface of the compost and the central portion of the clump either 'goes back' or flowers badly.

But whereas bulbous plants are moved at dormancy when the roots have died away, most alpines need to be separated either in early spring or mid-autumn. Evergreen species are always more difficult to handle – damage to the foliage is almost inevitable and an extra burden is placed on the root system. With dormant crowns, by contrast, the soil can be either washed off by immersion in a bucket of water or gingerly shaken off by prodding with a hand fork, pulling the crowns apart and taking off any damaged areas before holding the section in place, and trickling compost around and between the roots, checking for any signs of pests (particularly vine weevil) in so doing.

The divisions do not always come apart automatically, and a plant like *Primula allionii* will often need a judicious cut with a sharp knife, again treating the affected area with a fungicide. Before replanting, this exercise provides a chance to clear away dead basal leaves, old roots and (possibly) last year's spent capsules. Where the roots are thick, it often pays to dip them in water, shake off the excess and dredge them in dry silver sand before replanting. This is not practical where fibrous rooted species are concerned, but these seldom suffer a check in growth after the operation, and can be literally pulled apart, the number of divisions depending on the quantity of plants needed. Small rooted shoots that break off can be potted separately and nursed on until they begin to develop – these are so-called 'Irishman's cuttings'. Even if little of the root survives, new ones will generally appear when placed in fresh compost – something that is very noticeable with the genus *Soldanella*, where washing all the compost away from the roots will reveal a knotted mass of growth that can be broken up and the fragments potted individually in a peat-based compost, watered well, and grown on to provide plants that soon match the dimensions of their parent.

Root cuttings

The time of the year these can be taken varies somewhat, from early autumn for species of *Ranunculus* such as *R. calandrinioides*, through to mid/late winter (*Phlox mesoleuca*, several species of *Primula*), and on into the

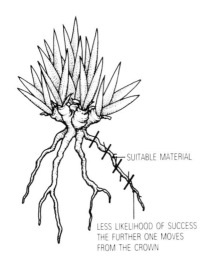

SUITABLE MATERIAL

LESS LIKELIHOOD OF SUCCESS
THE FURTHER ONE MOVES
FROM THE CROWN

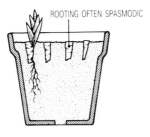

ROOTING OFTEN SPASMODIC

Figure 17   Root cuttings

spring with *Weldenia candida*, which is one of the few plants subjected to this treatment whilst still in growth.

The root system is exposed, and a few of the stronger ones (which have a substantial food reserve) cut off below the crown. Any finer tributary roots are trimmed off to leave a single thong perhaps 20cm long, which can be cut into sections at least 2–3cm long. These are traditionally cut horizontally across their upper end and diagonally across their lower, so that they can be inserted into pots of silver sand the same way up as when connected to the plant. The adventitious growth bud will develop from the top end, which needs to be level or just proud of the rooting medium surface – failure is very likely if they are planted the wrong way up.

Those cuttings taken from the top half of the root will be able to regenerate best, but with rare plants it is sensible to use all the material available. A fungicide is used, in either powder or water-based spray form, and the inserted cuttings covered with coarse grit. Subsequent watering is seldom necessary. Some people prefer to enclose the pot, which is filled with a very sandy compost, in a polythene bag to minimise water loss. The easiest plants to rear on this treatment, such as *Morisia monanthos*, will usually take a month after insertion in the early spring to be ready for moving into another pot, whereas plants started off in the autumn will seldom be ready before the temperature rises several months into the new year.

Leaf cuttings
Very few plants suitable for the alpine house are propagated by this method and of those that can be (several of the non-aestivating lewisias, for example) the infrequency with which this method is chosen shows that it is not a popular choice. Nevertheless, most of the Old World members of the Gesneriaceae can be increased in this way, though only *Ramonda myconi* appears with any great frequency. *Petrocosmea kerrii*, a useful late-flowering alpine in spite of its frost tenderness, will come readily from leaf cuttings, and the bigeneric hybrid × *Briggandra calliantha*, following the lead of its Japanese parent, gives reasonably good results.

With them all, compost is scraped away from the base of the rosette in the springtime, and the leaf detached by pulling downwards so that the petiole comes away with it in its entirety. A pot containing equal parts of peat and sand is prepared, the compost moistened, and the base of the cutting inserted to a depth of 1cm or less. It may be necessary to secure the cutting with a loop of bent wire. Placed under a propagator hood, the pot can be left until the new rosette begins to appear against the inner leaf base.

One reads that *Jankaea heldreichii* (Plate 3) can be increased in this way, but the few plants seen are generally micropropagated, raised from seed or from rooted side shoots that have been painstakingly detached and grown on.

Grafting

Again, a form of propagation of little relevance to the alpine house gardener, except in as much as it relates to several species of *Daphne*. By far the most important is *D. petraea* 'Grandiflora', although its less attractive hybrid with *D. striata* (*D. × thauma*) can be increased in the same way, and slow growing plants like *D. arbuscula*, *D. cneorum pygmaea* (Plate 14) and *D. jasminea* are occasionally grafted, though they will grow satisfactorily on their own roots.

The technique is to select young seedlings of (usually) *Daphne mezereum* or *D. tangutica* and decapitate them at ground level, below the cotyledons, creating a wedge graft by cutting vertically down the rootstock to a depth of approx 1cm, and inserting a branchlet (scion) of the chosen species of *Daphne*, which has been treated by exposing the cambium. This entails making a clean cut on either side, bringing the cutting to a taper and making sure it is kept scrupulously clean, inserting it into the cleft, matching the cambium up with that of the rootstock.

To keep it in place, the graft is bound with grafting tape (only available from specialist suppliers) or, as is now often preferred, strips of polythene film sold principally for culinary purposes. The timing of this operation is flexible – if late winter is chosen, then *Daphne petraea* 'Grandiflora' is often hampered by its abundant crop of flower buds – a problem overcome by waiting until mid-summer, when the weather should be warm enough to make the artificial heating preferable at the earlier date unnecessary.

Whilst this daphne is not much troubled by fungal diseases, a spray with a fungicide before the plants are placed beneath a propagator hood is a wise precaution. The high humidity appears to be a material help until the graft takes (usually a month or so after the initial operation), after which increasing ventilation can be introduced.

Micropropagation

Since *in vitro* propagation is now showing signs of spreading beyond specialist laboratories into the domain of the informed amateur, a brief review is called for. We have already seen a variety of alpines coming onto the market via this process – previously scarce plants like *Primula aureata*, distinctive clones of *Lewisia cotyledon*, *Primula allionii*, × *Jankaemonda vandedemii* and a couple

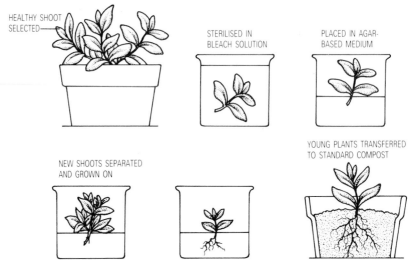

Figure 18   Micropropagation (a simplified version)

of the rarer species of *Dionysia* have all appeared in the 1980s, and doubtless this range is set to expand.

The basic concept involves taking small pieces of actively growing plant tissue (predominantly the shoot tip and sections of the stem or, with bulbs, the base of the scale leaves) and culturing them on nutrient agar under sterile conditions. Hygiene is vital, for in such closed conditions any contamination by bacteria or fungal spores will soon spread. To this end, the material chosen is first sterilised in a very weak bleach solution, and then rinsed in sterile water, before being placed on the agar in a flask, with controlled light and temperature. Depending on the site from which the propagating material came, it is either left relatively intact (pieces up to 1cm long), or in meristem culture, all extraneous material being removed with the probable aid of a dissecting microscope.

After several weeks in the initial nutrient base, the mass of plantlets formed are divided up, placed in separate flasks, and this process combined repeatedly to bulk up the numbers. From these the small plants are again removed onto a fresh agar bed, where the nutrient level will usually have been lowered. Roots will be expected to have formed in a matter of a few weeks: the sign to now persuade the young plants to grow in a conventional compost (nearly always peat based) and to phase in the normal environment in which the plant will live.

So far, the principal drawback has been that each species requires a different balance of nutrient levels and plant hormones (auxins and cytokinins). We are also seeing mutations, most clearly in the fasciation of certain North American species of *Fritillaria* – a problem associated with the use of callus, which forms when hormone levels in the flask are increased and is really just a mass of undifferentiated tissue.

11 Deciding What to Choose

Any collection of alpines tends to be a highly individual affair. Differences in local climate, availability of plants, small-scale exchange between like-minded enthusiasts, aptitude, and willingness to look beyond commercial sources: these factors create innumerable opportunities to select and, in time, to specialise. Yet, although one could point to a number of growers who have excelled in the cultivation of a particular genus, it is equally true that for as long as the alpine house has been popular, certain plants have found their way onto its benches with unfailing consistency. In a branch of gardening where many introductions come and go within a few years, this is surely an indication of their especial worth.

For those new to alpine house cultivation, and perhaps wondering exactly which plants might be suitable, it is not always easy to decide between the large selection on offer. The expression 'beginners' plants' is often introduced at this stage, but it seems to be an irrelevant one. First, plants so termed are to be found in the gardens of hobbyists of long standing, and secondly, initial collections increasingly include unusual and highly specialised alpines.

To start with, though, the choice will lie with those alpines in general cultivation. Their often lengthy history in our gardens is testimony both to the breadth of their appeal and their tolerance of the conditions we can provide. One or two might require that you put your name down on a nurseryman's waiting list, or raise the stock from seed, but possession does not presuppose the years of searching that ownership of their more *avant-garde* relatives sometimes involves.

Plants which are once in a while seen under glass, but have no need of such protection at any stage of the year – dwarf conifers, for example – have not been considered.

The basic collection

In the popular imagination, alpines are spring-flowering, but for many the season begins much earlier, when the first of the summer dormant corms and bulbs awaken in response to cooler night-time temperatures and, it would seem with some, an innate timing mechanism.

Autumn colour
By late summer/early autumn, several species of *Cyclamen* are coming to their best, and of those that do better kept in a pot than planted in the garden *C. mirabile* is outstanding. Coming from southwestern Turkey, one might expect it to be one of the less hardy species, but this has not been the case, although a

severe winter can lead to defoliation. The most distinctive feature of the flowers is the toothing at the apex of the petals. When corms first came into general cultivations in the mid 1960s many had pale pink blooms, but more recently bluish pink forms have appeared. It is desirable, but seldom possible, to choose from flowering specimens. For anyone who is not conversant with the controversy over wild imported cyclamen, it is sufficient to advise that plants are best obtained in growth from a reputable supplier – those roughly dug, overdried corms from the former source cause much disappointment when they fail to grow and have given the genus an undeserved reputation for being temperamental. The compost chosen should be friable, well-drained and amply provided with humus. Most of the species grow on limestone formations, and an annual dressing of bonemeal seems to be appreciated. For the dormant period, the pot can be removed to a covered, shaded frame and kept barely moist, treatment which also suits one of the finest spring-flowering representatives, *C. pseudibericum*. Although the corm forms a surprisingly extensive root system, it is recommended that the container chosen should be of the minimum size necessary to accommodate it: overpotting is inadvisable. An elderly corm of this species may be little more than 6–8cm across, and after the first few years it is often better to knock it out of the pot at dormancy and replace the compost before rehousing it in a similar sized pot. This need not be an annual event.

Another genus that spreads its flowering season over a similar period is *Narcissus*, and depending on the severity of the winter, it is possible to bring colour to the alpine house even in the bleakness of early winter. Ignoring the spasmodically available – and more important, spasmodically flowering – autumnal species of the Mediterranean, we come quickly to the Bulbocodium section, and the cream hoop petticoats of *N. cantabricus foliosus* – one of several Moroccan representatives that in some years will bloom even in the early autumn. Outside, the long and wiry leaves are soon disposed of by slugs, and the 2cm-long flowers are held back long enough to catch the worst of the autumn rains. Moreover, they really do seem to appreciate a warm summer rest, and increase remarkably swiftly when these conditions prevail.

The majority of the widely available spring-flowering daffodils are more effective planted in the garden but *N. rupicola* from the central sierras of Spain seldom forms the flowery clumps that one expects of pot-grown examples, even when provided with a stony loam and a raised position. The single, jonquil-shaped flowers can scent the whole greenhouse and measure up to 2.5cm across – not that the size of the flower necessarily makes for what is loosely called a 'good' form. This species sets seed very freely, and the bulbs can be relied upon to flower annually, rather than splitting into a mass of immature bulbils in the way that several of the true Jonquils are wont to do.

Spring

From bulbs the attention shifts to the first evergreen plants, and by the New Year the flower buds of the Porophyllum saxifrages are usually well formed.

Nearly all the species – and the innumerable hybrids – of this section are better grown outdoors for much of the year, but flowering so early, and at a time when the birds take particular delight in pecking at them mercilessly, they make a vivid display under glass. Interest in growing them has been rekindled in the wake of a new generation of hybrids produced in the USA, Czechoslovakia and most recently the UK but one of the best, *Saxifraga burseriana* 'Gloria', is also one of the oldest, dating back to the turn of the century. The spiny, grey-green rosettes form a regular cushion that is attractive throughout the year, but when in February or early March this is hidden beneath a swathe of large white blooms the true worth of the plant is revealed. At this flowering time, full light is needed, but by mid-summer gardeners in warmer areas find that even grown outside, some shading may be necessary to prevent scorching. There is some dispute here, with the suggestion that scorching only occurs when the plants are insufficiently moist, but with larger cushions it pays to be wary on this matter. Many of these saxifrages, popularly known as the Kabschia group, fell from favour because with age they flowered less freely, but this and indeed most of the clones of *S. burseriana* have no such failing, although if kept too dry over the winter months the flower buds will abort.

Increasing exploration of the Himalayan chain, where this section is well represented, has brought to our gardens several attractive species new to cultivation, but one hesitates to recommend them as yet for a preliminary collection. The exception is *Saxifraga poluniniana*, probably first successfully introduced as recently as 1981, but already well established in cultivation, seeding freely and siring a number of promising hybrids. The small flowers, slightly oval in shape like most of the species from these mountains, open white but fade over the course of a fortnight to pink, and are borne on very short stems scarcely above the foliage. Any suspicion of dryness during the growing season can be disastrous.

Another of the backbone genera for the rock plant enthusiast, *Primula*, provides us with perhaps the archetypal alpine house plant, *P. allionii*. Growing wild in the Maritime Alps, usually at quite modest altitudes, the dense mounds of slightly sticky rosettes tend to be isolated from other vegetation, usually growing out of vertical crevices in the limestone or even positioned upside down in cave entrances. Overhead watering is tolerated if a warm, drying wind happens to be blowing, but there is usually a risk attached, particularly as the cushion builds up. It is hard to remember ever having seen a good plant out of doors, although small specimens may continue to grow for a number of years if cunningly sighted away from driving rain.

For some reason, it is unusual for amateurs to raise this species from seed, possibly because several of the clones enjoy an almost unassailable popularity, or perhaps because the seed capsules are difficult to find tucked away near the centre of the rosette and take an inordinately long time to ripen. The normal experience is to purchase a plant with just a single rosette, and wait a minimum of some five years before it can be brought to satisfactory maturity. From then on, accidents apart, the cushions can be coaxed in some cases to fill a 30 cm pot, although the speed with which this happens varies markedly according to the clone. Similarly, it is generally claimed that the cushions completely cover themselves with flower, whereas this character too is very variable, and does not depend simply upon the standard of cultivation. Of the named forms, the purple pink variety *P.a.* 'Crowsley', paler and white eyed 'Marion', 'Fanfare' (whose leaves are distinctively toothed, whereas the majority have an entire leaf margin), and the very large flowered 'Elliotts Var.' (also sold as 'KRW form' and 'grandiflora') can be relied upon to flower profusely. Availability of these clones is uneven, and there are numerous plants without a cultivar name that perform equally well.

By mid-April, when the main two-month flowering period is complete, it becomes necessary to remove the spent blooms, which otherwise decompose around the tender new growth, causing fungal infection within a matter of days. For much the same reason, it helps to raise the cushion off the surface of the compost with some flakes of a 'hard' limestone – absorbent material such as tufa is seldom as satisfactory. There has been a recent upswing in interest surrounding hybrids with other European species, these being more tolerant of overhead moisture and faster growing. *P. marginata* has been the favoured match (the two hybridise in the wild on occasion) and the resultant hybrids, identified as *P.* × *miniera*, tend to be characterised by richly coloured flowers on longer scapes, often inheriting the attractive farina covered leaves of the pollen plant. Going a stage further, hybrids of *P. marginata* itself have been bred into *P. allionii* but unfortunately a proportion of the stocks (*P.* 'Beatrice Wooster', for instance) have become badly virused. If grown alongside 'clean' stock, there is always the possibility that the condition will spread to others in the group.

Despite the large number of horticulturally significant species contained in the genus *Primula*, it has to be said that relatively few – certainly of the widely grown members – can be recommended. They dislike the low humidity and well-lit conditions that prevail in the summer, by which time many have grown greatly expanded leaves that the roots find it difficult to keep properly supplied in a heatwave. However, one of the American species, *P. ellisiae*, because it remains dormant until quite late in the spring and is really better glass-covered when at rest, is now well established as an alpine house plant, where the one-sided umbels of rose-coloured flowers appear in late spring, among or slightly above the rather narrow, well-developed leaves. As with the foregoing species, a slightly shaded position is preferable once flowering is complete, but it differs in needing a large root run and a humus-rich compost. Although owners of several plants find that seed sets readily in cultivation, recent sendings from its New Mexico habitats have served to emphasise the degree of variation in the appearance of the flower. A clear white form has long been grown, but remains a very rare plant.

Included in *Primula* by some taxonomists, the cushion-forming Dionysias centred in the mountains of Iran and Afghanistan, possibly reached their zenith in our gardens in the wake of fruitful expeditions to those countries in the 1960s and early 1970s. The majority have persisted, though often in very small numbers, but only *Dionysia aretioides*, from the Elburz Mountains to the north of Tehran, has met with widespread success. When well grown, the downy aromatic cushions can be completely obscured in early spring by long tubed, miniature 'primroses', which vary in depth of colour but are usually golden yellow. Several cultivars have been identified, the position confused since it has been possible to induce seed set and the resulting plants can end up with their parents clonal name attached . . . something that unfortunately holds true with numerous other genera.

Given the painfully slow rate of many of the species, the steady increase that can be expected of *D. aretioides* suggests different treatment. Repotting is likely to be necessary at least once a year to begin with, the root damage always warned against tending to occur when a specimen becomes potbound. A compost comprising 50 per cent chippings and equal parts loam and peat has proved satisfactory. If using the John Innes formulation, then there is a move towards No. 3, since cases where the plants are suffering from starvation have been diagnosed. Along with overwatering during the winter, this is likely to be the reason for many of the casualties, and in view of the species' capacity to form a cushion well over 30cm across after 6–8 years, growing a plant or two on an open bed within the alpine house (see Chapter 9) is a logical step. One word of warning – when at rest the plant can look very untidy, with the dead outer leaves of each rosette clasped against the small green centre. This is normal behaviour and need not give cause for concern.

The numerous species of *Androsace* exert a similar appeal, and although widely distributed across the mountains of the northen hemisphere, it is the European species that have retained their popularity. Of those that inhabit rock fissures and form a tight mat or dome, the most suitable is probably *A. vandellii*, which is tolerant enough of warm summers to extend its range south to the Sierra Nevada and across to the High Atlas. In the wild, one finds it growing in the cracks of massively jointed granite formations, the largest plants usually shaded from the midday sun, and assuming watering is not neglected similarly spartan treatment can yield good results in the garden.

At one stage, it was thought appropriate to grow a wide range of high alpines in a very lean compost (normally given as three parts grit to one part peat/leafmould), and for plants such as the androsace this remains excellent advice. The cushions can be increased more speedily in a richer compost, but the price is usually a shorter-lived, less compact specimen. One should remember with plants brought from a supplier that the adjustment to a more spartan regime is not always successful. With young plants it is usual to ease as much as possible of the old compost away from the roots before carefully working in the new, but by raising a batch of seedlings this problem is side-stepped, besides which one is likely to end up with plants exhibiting different characteristics, both of vigour and general appearance.

This is equally true of *A. cylindrica* × *hirtella*, whose rather similar white flowers, produced on tiny pedicels from the leaf axils, can be abundant enough

95

to rest in a double layer over the dark green cushions. Longevity is a subject often glossed over with these plants, but the average age of a specimen at maturity is between five and ten years. It is here that some of the Asiatic species score, particularly those that spread strawberry-like from stolons, the rosettes rooting down where they touch the ground instead of being dependent upon a single rootstock. Several of them cannot be relied upon to flower freely, and comparing the foliage of cultivated plants with their counterparts in the wild this can be attributed to an over-rich compost in many cases. One of the better species, *A. villosa* var. *jacquemontii*, introduces vivid purple-pink to the range of colours, and is simplicity itself to propagate by detaching a few of the peripheral rosettes after flowering. In time, it forms an even silky-haired mat which benefits from glass protection during the winter, this also preventing birds from selecting it for nesting material in the spring. The choice of topdressing calls for some attention, for unless a fairly fine grade of grit is used (washed quartz graded up to 5mm is ideal) then rooting will be inhibited.

Before leaving the cushion plants, a word should be said about one of the longest lived, *Draba mollissima*, a species which is still represented by material that can be traced back over 50 years: there appears to be no record of a more recent introduction. One suspects that the size of the plant is controlled in later life by availability of large pots. Moreover, it is probable that poor flowering from these massive growths, 30cm or more across, results from being left year after year in the same container, and this is one of the few instances where liquid feeding becomes essential rather than an optional extra. Watering needs to be carefully controlled from the moment the close grey-green dome shows signs of dormancy in mid autumn until the bright green new growth, peppered with tiny yellow flower buds, begins to advance, but the massive root system must be kept adequately supplied thereafter. Watering around the side of the plant does not always achieve this, and to remove any doubt, with plants over roughly 15cm across, it is beneficial to immerse the pot to half its depth in a bucket of water, leaving it there ten minutes until the compost is thoroughly soaked. Because you have surfaced the pan with coarse chippings to a depth of at least 3cm, the woolly foliage will have a dry (or at least quick drying) base on which to rest.

Varying needs

The flowers of the draba are attractive *en masse*, but curious rather than beautiful close to, and it is I think broadly true that for many alpine house enthusiasts, an interest in the specialised, on occasions bizarre adaptions of plants to their environment runs parallel with an appreciation of their beauty. *Lewisia* satisfies both these demands, for the thick fleshy foliage typical of most members reflects their summer as surely as the aestivating habit of the remainder. The latter are exemplified by *L. rediviva*, which although long lived will never need a large pot, seed being the primary means of increase. The narrow leaves first appear in the early autumn, but not until the following year in late spring do the showy flowers – up to 5cm across and ranging in colour from deep rose pink to ivory white – open out if a warm, sunny day presents itself. Like most of the genus, annual repotting is recommended. Very early spring is probably the best time to do this. Whilst these plants have been grown in limestone areas, it is more satisfactory to aim for a pH of 7 or slightly less, selecting a rich loam mixed with an equal quantity of grit.

Those species that die down after flowering need to be kept dry until growth restarts two or three months later. Doubtless some gardeners have kept plants outdoors for the summer with no ill effects on occasion, but these are exceptions that prove the general rule. It is as well to add that those which retain their foliage, generally growing in areas where high summer rainfall is sparse, do not dry out to the same extent, and the skill lies in keeping the compost barely moist in hot weather. Trying to compensate by watering heavily nearly always causes the caudex to rot, although a really deep topdressing, down the carrot-like neck to the point where the root begins to branch, will lessen the risk. One of the favourites, *L. tweedyi*, is also the earliest flowering, and we now have colour variations said to be unknown in the Wenatchee Mountains of Washington from whence the species originates – everything from a good pink through pale rose shot through with yellow or apricot and on to white.

More readily come by, and robust enough for garden use, although they normally achieve greater longevity where rain cannot lodge at the leafbases, are the large numbers of variants of *Lewisia cotyledon*. The more strident colours that are often to be seen – mustard yellow, orange and cerise – are very much an acquired taste, and the freely produced shiny black seed, sown for preference as soon as it ripens, has seen the establishment of several strains. The subtler shades of pink and the white forms are well worth searching out. This species has been mated with various others and the literature is replete with the names of defunct hybrids, which is a powerful argument against recommending any of those currently on offer.

The lewisias are at their best in late spring, and this time of year also sees the flowering of one of the classic alpine shrubs, *Daphne petraea* 'Grandiflora'. This clone is seen almost to the exclusion of the unselected species, and most of the plants in cultivation are grafted onto rootstocks of *D. mezereum*, which encourages faster growth. Daphnes grown under glass have a reputation for dying with inexplicable suddenness and defoliating in the summer: the results of the compost drying out (which the plants seldom tolerate) and red spider mite. Failing to regulate the watering properly is also the reason that some plants fail to flower . . . the buds are set by early autumn, but will abort if the roots are not kept moist. Growth is most vigorous just after flowering, and this is the best time to repot – not difficult with young plants, but always something of a gamble when a large plant is involved. None the less, plants well into their second and third decade are still being grown, and the one-time rarity of the species reflected the nurseryman's understandable reluctance to propagate in the face of a negligible economic gain.

It is with some hesitation that *Gentiana* is included here, although it provides the alpine gardener with some of the most attractive plants he or she could wish for. Few of those widely grown, it has to be said, are suitable for the alpine house. However, *Gentiana verna* v. *angulosa* has been grown superbly in this way, and once such a plant has provided the encouragement, less experienced gardeners may be stimulated to increase the range of plants that they grow, in the process transferring to the garden any species there is no specific reason to retain under glass.

If the right site cannot be contrived in the garden, of course, then keeping a plant in the greenhouse is often the only means of growing it to an acceptable standard. *Ramonda myconi* is a plant that takes to life in a pot with alacrity, and for much of the year can be placed in the poorest-lit areas where many other occupants would quickly become etiolated. When seen growing along moist cliff ledges in the Pyrenees, there is often some shade cast by surrounding trees and shrubs, or if the site is free of this growth, then the sun usually strikes for only a few hours due to the aspect chosen. To counteract the drying atmosphere, overhead watering is desirable in the growing period, for the large leaves soon dry up and show damage along their margins. Unlike the majority of alpines, an application of nitrogen-based liquid feed after flowering can benefit the plant without inducing atypical growth or, worse still, causing damage – something that can happen with plants native to soils where supplies of this element are low.

Some plants we retain in the alpine house not so much to stave off the effect of the climate as to protect them from pest damage. The slug is probably the greatest offender, and one of the first targets is likely to be *Soldanella alpina*, one of a small genus whose delicate fringed bells are familiar throughout much of the European alpine system, decorating the matted turf near to the melting snow or, in the case of several species, growing by the thousand in the upper woodlands. Opinion is divided, but one suspects that they grow best in a soilless compost, spreading by a network of runners at or just below the surface to form a mat, which experience shows it is best to divide at regular intervals, since the ratio of flower to foliage tends to fall away for every year that the move is delayed. There are exceptions, and one satisfactory dodge is to replant a number of divisions just slightly apart where, with luck, they will run into one another and flower freely for a couple of seasons. It is perhaps significant that natural stands of *S. alpina* are predominantly composed of small plants, individuals with between five and eleven spikes (the maximum observed) being very much in the minority. The other factor to bear in mind is that at flowering time, and often long afterwards, the ground is soaking wet: it is almost impossible to overwater a soldanella once growth is under way. In my experience, keeping the plants under glass, but still moist at the roots, has consistently led to better flowering.

Also favoured by the slug, *Physoplexis comosa* seldom looks at its best in a pot, whereas growing out of a hole in a lump of tufa its appearance is transformed. Some plants are far more readily disposed to increase their number of crowns than others, and because of its reputation, patently inferior seedlings are sometimes offered on the strength of the name alone. When it retires for the winter, its completely deciduous nature can fool you into thinking that a death has taken place, but the moisture drawn up from the surrounding plunge will be enough to prompt the young, crimson red shoots into growth early in the spring. By early summer, an established plant can carry upwards of a dozen of the unmistakable compound flowerheads.

Its close cousin *Campanula* is another staple of the rock garden that provides several species whose safety one fears for in the open. This holds true not only of the frequently monocarpic Mediterranean species but of those from the higher mountains, their generous blooming habit providing a welcome lift in the alpine house when so many of the occupants have long since finished flowering. For sheer individuality, the constricted bells of *C. zoysii* are unmatched: the tufts of tiny ovate leaves expanding (rarely) to 30cm across and covering themselves with bloom. Reports of plants growing wild in the Karawanken Mountains and elsewhere indicate rather smaller specimens, usually threading their way through vertical limestone crevices, and presenting themselves in all shades of blue – a diversity only recently seen in garden stocks. After such a display, it is probably best to cut off all traces of flower, apply a *weak* dose of low nitrogen fertiliser, and at the first sign of new growth lift the plant out of its pot onto a worksurface, teasing as many rooted pieces from the tangle as possible and planting them in a standard potting compost (see Chapter 6) that incorporates some limestone chippings. Most clones show this suckering habit, and as with other species it is an indication that failure to carry out division may result in the old central portion drying out, this process spreading to the outer portions as the compost gives up its nutrients. Slow-release fertilisers offer limited help, and plants given winter cover grow well outside the alpine house, though sooner or later a slug usually brings such ventures to an end.

Strangely, the robust hybrid between *C. raineri* and *C. morettiana*, 'Joe Elliott' is less affected by being root bound once a reasonable sized (10cm+) plant has been achieved. As an experiment, a plant was left for five years in the same container, the only real attention being an annual clean up in late winter, just before it came into leaf, when the topdressing was carefully brushed off the network of fragile stems, any obviously dead growth discarded and a dressing of bonemeal applied before replacing with up to 3cm of fine limestone grit. The gritty compost and well-lit position necessitated quite copious watering but the effort resulted in an astonishing display of the large mid-blue bells, as many as five on each short stem, produced in a quantity and with a regularity that is only rarely seen in either of the parents. Outdoors, the flowers are badly marked by rain.

Flowering at much the same time, and continuing to produce the odd bloom until the first frosts, the plant known to generations of gardeners as *Phlox mesoleuca* has gained ground in cultivation now that the myth that it can be propagated only by root cuttings has been laid to rest. Its rhizomatous nature is sometimes demonstrated when the roots of pot-grown plants range through the drainage hole, and looking across the plunge, new shoots can be seen pushing through over a wide area. If the woody topgrowth is retained during winter dormancy, growth will occasionally resume both here and at ground level, but the natural propensity of the species to ramble persuades most owners to clip off the old stems in late autumn. Several other collections of these Protophlox from the Mexican end of their distribution have expanded the colour range from the clear pink of the original to include red, yellow and white. Some can be artificially pollinated to produce viable seed even in a comparatively cool climate. Planted out in the alpine house, they are usually happier than when grown in the open, where frosting of the spring growth is a problem, particularly in alternation with heavy falls of rain. At one time, this vulnerability was confused with a general inability to tolerate low temperatures, and the way in which weak, badly treated or borderline plants succumb depending on their positioning and the timing of the cold snap can lead to unjustified accusations of tenderness.

Orchids like *Pleione limprichtii* have withstood mid-winter temperatures of −25°C when kept dry underneath the staging of the alpine house, notwithstanding the early appearance of flowering buds from the base of the pseudo bulb. Annual repotting in the early spring provides the opportunity to grow on the offsets, and space those of flowering size to prevent an overcrowded appearance. Part of the misunderstanding may have arisen because others of the genus are sold as windowsill plants, and moreover some of them – the widely admired, lemon-yellow *P.* × *confusa* for example – can be killed outright by a hard frost. The species mentioned is troublefree if grown in a peat-based compost and kept moist during the summer, spraying the leaves with water and utilising the shadiest position possible, or by removing the pan to a similarly illuminated site outside once the flowers are spent in late spring.

The same injustice has been dealt to *Rhodohypoxis baurii*; this was introduced into cultivation in 1877 from the Drakensberg, but made popular in a range of named seedlings, pink, red and white, worked up from an unidentified, dessicated stock sent to England in the 1920s. As with so many alpine plants, one person took up their cause and through the attention that only a specialist would devote, Mrs Garnett-Bottfield worked up a stock that ran into thousands of plants. Like many bulbs, they will tolerate winter wet but can be killed by low temperatures when grown in an unplunged pot if the compost is frozen. Flowering can be controlled by starting them into growth in a warm room – something many alpine gardeners find a distasteful practice but which extends the normal late spring/early summer blooming period.

Mention of a plant from southern Africa provides the opportunity to observe that several species from this area have found alpine house conditions to their liking. When nothing else is in flower, we can still admire the silvery white carpet of *Helichrysum milfordiae*, which when suited takes up more space than the average alpine house can allow, but is ornamental the year round, something one can hardly say of outdoor specimens in a sodden winter. The distinctive, everlasting flowers can be freely produced, and like several of the genus this becomes more likely when planted in tufa, a method which inhibits vegetative increase taking place at the expense of flowers.

Its place under glass is likely to be supplanted by *H. pagophilum* whose horticulturally irrelevant flowers are more than made up for by an ease in cultivation that offsets the challenge presented by other elements of the collection. The rosettes are much smaller than those of *H. milfordiae*, seldom more than 2cm across and huddled into a tight dome that can reach up to 1m in its Lesotho homeland. So far, a compost made of equal parts peat, lime-free grit and loam has worked well, but the plant is likely to be easily suited, provided it is kept moist enough to prevent yellowing of the lower leaves in the summer.

12 Plants and Preferences

Having suggested a nucleus of plants that most alpine house owners are likely to attempt at one time or another, we are faced with a choice of thousands more, some regularly offered and others likely to be so or perhaps available just once in the course of a lifetime. Rather than compile an alphabetical list, it is proposed to discuss the more important categories of alpine plants normally accorded protection, illustrating with reference to appropriate species. Naturally it would be possible to place numerous alpines under several of these headings. Qualifying on one count is reason enough to make alpine house cultivation a viable option: more than this and the point is merely underlined.

It is appreciated that the area where the owner lives will influence considerably what can and cannot be grown. Examples of alpine houses are to be found in various parts of the USA and of Canada; in Scandinavia and from the UK through to continental Europe; in Japan, Australia, New Zealand and doubtless other countries too. The considerable climatic differences implicit will dictate which uses are of greatest importance.

Plants difficult to cultivate

At the outset it needs to be established that this subject has many faces. There are degrees of difficulty: unresolved complications relating to the way a plant performs in our gardens varying from an inability to grow as we would wish to an inability to grow at all. It is not unusual for a plant to pose problems when it is first brought into cultivation, but these can frequently be resolved as we become more familiar with its normal pattern of growth, clues often being found in the conditions prevailing in its native habitat.

More worrying are those plants that have been attempted by generations of gardeners, the material derived from right across their natural distribution, which have traditionally met with little or no success. In that they repeatedly occur naturally alongside perfectly easily cultivated species, there are less clues to explain their reluctance. *Eritrichium nanum*, whose variants crop up in several mountainous and arctic regions of the northern hemisphere, almost never attains the floriferousness and longevity that holds true in some of its wild stands. Seed germinates well, and young plants of certain representatives, notably ssp. *jankae* from Romania's Bucegi Mountains and what is styled *E. aretioides* from the Rocky Mountains, are more readily brought to a first flowering than others. Here their story normally ends. Another puzzle is that if

102

15. *Gentiana verna*

16. *Helichrysum pagophilum*

17. *Lewisia pygmaea*

18. *Narcissus rupicola*

19. *Ranunculus parnassifolius* 'Pink Form

20. *Viola calcarata*

cuttings are taken, the parent plant sometimes falls into an almost immediate decline.

Fortunately, it is more usually the case that we can identify the reason(s) for their difficulty, though not necessarily be able to right matters. It is now appreciated that the highest growing alpines (those whose lowest recorded height is 4,000m or more) seldom grow well at lower altitudes, their discomfort being readily apparent in the warmer summer months. This holds true of most, if not all of the great mountain ranges – think of *Gentiana urnula* growing at over 6,000m in Nepal, *Arenaria glanduligera* which becomes loose and abandons its attractive, floriferous normal habit, *Trifolium nanum* (a hard bun in the wild; a loose growing plant in the garden, how ever much you restrict its diet) and *Phlox condensata*, which in lowland sites becomes both etiolated and much less floriferous. Temperature is likely to be just as important as the increased levels of ultra violet light – witness how European alpines like *Ranunculus glacialis* and *Androsace glacialis* prefer to spend the summer in the open garden, their foliage pleasingly compact when compared with alpine house specimens, and flowering in some instances comparable with that of a healthy wild plant.

Not only the summer, but moreover the winter temperature may rise too high. Because they grow at such extreme altitudes, snow cover is more reliable (barring cliff-dwelling species) and comes much earlier. Lowland winters, conversely, usually allow unseasonal growth, which may be at the expense of flower formation. The poor light levels make matters worse and lead to weak growth: the high growing alpines do not always escape dense palls of mists and cloud cover, but when the sun does break through, it is intense.

Putting aside the matter of specific clones that flower sparsely, non-blooming is part of the question of what makes an alpine plant difficult to grow well in the alpine house. Plants such as *Viola calcarata* (Plate 20) have long been known to fail in this respect, and observations suggest that this is more pronounced when the compost is too wet, where upon the buds turn yellow and fail to develop. Others actually seem to need copious watering if flower buds are to promote themselves – in the wild, poor flowering follows on from sparse snowfall that results in comparatively low moisture levels in the spring. *Aquilegia jonesii* can sometimes be persuaded to respond to this treatment.

These are all plants that have proved generally difficult to grow well; they appear to be less forgiving of the mistakes that even the most skilled gardeners make all the time. For this reason those who grow them invariably take an interest in their propagation, if only to lengthen the odds against repeating the same mistake and wiping out all the stock.

Numerous other plants are classed as difficult, but have been grown extremely well in the alpine houses of those prepared to devote extra time to their specific needs. With the many choice pulvinate *Astragalus* introduced from the western USA and Turkey, hatred of root disturbance has been dealt with by sowing seeds individually, one to each small pot, which avoids the pricking out that this genus on the whole loathes. The woody rootstock that develops after the first couple of years is an indication of their resistance to low summer rainfall – the majority of the more interesting ones inhabit semi-desert conditions, and with species such as *A. aretioides* and *A. coccineus*, the white felted foliage needs glass protection and abundant ventilation if it is not to succumb.

This remains true of the majority of dionysias known in our gardens. Even when their root run remains moist, the foliage is invariably shaded from rainfall, since most occur on limestone cliffs, with the protected rockface behind an overhang a favoured site. Long lived in these positions, a number have been grown to a respectable size and age in specialist collections, although most are unforgiving of any maltreatment, so that apart from *Dionysia curviflora*, specimens over ten years old are rarely seen.

None the less, techniques of handling have now improved to the extent that healthy mounds of *D. tapetodes* overlapping a 30cm pot and, in some years, flowering very freely, have been produced. The realisation that clonal selection can produce relatively well-tempered forms of 'difficult' plants has been of importance – with the latter species, for example, it is usually found that plants with farinose leaves grow more reliably than their efarinose counterparts. Although there are exceptions, the likelihood is that dionysias grow best under conditions of light summer shade, and farinose forms of *D. tapetodes* may simply be less prone to scorch.

Those species that despite repeated introductions do not usually grow well in cultivation can be specifically adapted to cope with their environment. Of the dionysias, *D. michauxii* is obviously not subjected to long periods of damp, cold weather or summer spells of high humidity in its very specific type locality in southwest Iran, and looking for a moment at the lesser known species, it tends to be those restricted to a very specific niche or equipped with hairy leaves that resist attempts to grow them. If seed can be persuaded to set, then variation in vigour, floriferousness and general form can be expected, and line breeding can in time lead to strains more tolerant of garden conditions. Unfortunately, the majority of the rarer dionysias are represented in cultivation by either single or incompatible clones, and being predominantly heterostylous this possibility awaits the renewed introduction of wild material.

A last comment on the factors limiting the ease with which 'difficult' plants adapt to cultivation: we are attempting to grow these species well outside their natural range, and if the gap between what can be offered in the alpine house and what the plants are accustomed to when growing wild is too wide, it is hardly surprising that they expire. A limit as expressed in the minimum altitude or southernmost latitude of a given species can often be related to temperature rather than rainfall, soil type or suitable terrain. If this is the case, then providing a suitable compost and devising an appropriate watering regime may not be enough. Their metabolism is highly temperature-sensitive in many instances, and if it cannot be regulated, then a warm spell will mean that the plants' respiration rate rises considerably, using up carbohydrate (stored in the leaves) and leading to the collapse of the plant through what alpine gardeners used to call 'overheating' if usage outstrips the level of replacement. An unusually warm summer can wreak havoc, both weakening plants to the stage where they succumb to secondary attack by pests and diseases, and after years of successful cultivation killing some outright.

Recent introductions

The alpine house is a place to experiment. It is almost in the nature of this form of gardening that whilst stopping periodically to appreciate the beauty of the plants grown, a desire to improve our efforts leaves little room for complacency. Investigating the possibilities that lie untapped in unfamiliar species not only provides added interest and a sense of achievement when the method of growing the plant proves rewarding, but invariably also provides clues on ways of bettering our treatment of more familiar fare.

When travel to the world's mountainous regions involved lengthy sea passages, weeks of trekking over sketchily chartered territory before even the foothills were reached, and then exploratory seed collection not confined to alpine levels, it was usually true that whatever found its way back home more than likely ended up at the botanic garden that had devised the expedition or among a small number of subscribers. The pathways to wider distribution were limited, apart from which the number of people wishing to grow such plants was, by present-day standards, restricted to a handful. Some 20 or 30 years after its initial germination in someone's alpine house, it was still possible to refer to a plant as being a novelty.

This has all changed. With modern air travel making it possible to travel half way across the world within a day, and communications on the ground reaching once-remote ranges, little- known plants have been introduced (albeit often on a local scale and rather haphazardly) in an unparalleled diversity. And the rise in membership of the relevant specialist societies, which have by turns both mirrored and encouraged this wider interest, provides a network down which new plants, or at least some of them, can be filtered.

Species never previously cultivated, and in rare instances completely new to science, can pass from itinerant enthusiast to specialist/nurseryman and on into commerce within a few short months. A conspicuously successful example has been *Clematis marmoraria*, known only from a couple of mountains in South Island, New Zealand and discovered as recently as 1970. Some ten years later the first plants became horticulturally established in its native country. However, it took only a further one or two years before material from various sources could be found in alpine houses up and down the British Isles, and beyond that a similar period until the knack of obtaining floriferous specimens was achieved and second generation seedlings began to spread around, not in small quantities but by the hundred. By this time it had been established that:

(1) Although found growing on marble in its wild state, limestone need not be added to the compost and could cause chlorosis.

(2) The plant was adaptable to both soil and peat-based composts, but preferred the latter, in keeping with the well drained fissures, filled with a near neutral humus-rich medium, of its habitat.

(3) It was frost hardy but did not enjoy cold wet winters; whilst in growth it needed ample watering, and had a large, branching root system that necessitated frequent repotting.

(4) Some seedlings were stoloniferous, and there were apparent differences in the ease with which male and female plants could be grown.

(5) Propagation was straightforward by internodal cuttings taken at any time in the summer, or if both sexes were available then from seed, sown fresh to prevent a dormancy not broken by the first seasons' winter chilling. Hybrids with other New Zealand species (at least four to date) appeared.

(6) The firm dark green leaflets attracted few pests, although the slow to develop flower buds were sometimes infested with aphids.

Unfortunately, for every plant that proves its worth in our gardens, can be propagated by several means and induced both to grow and flower as well as could be wished, there are a hundred of others that die after an unremitting struggle to keep them alive or, if they live, fail to retain the features that made it seem a good idea to attempt to bring them into cultivation. An appreciation of their normal lifespan, pattern of growth and overall environment cannot always be relied upon to inform our attempts to grow them in every last detail. What such knowledge *can* do is to let us know what to aim for in their appearance, and where to make a start (compost, watering, aspect) towards that end.

There will always be isolated successes from time to time, but it is a gradual, collective appreciation of alpine plants' varying requirements that underpins the establishment of unfamiliar species. This may well be why flowering plants of *Oreopolus glacialis*, which are local but not infrequent in the southern Andes, have now been raised, following years of general failure. Learning of the stable slightly acidic, sandy screes in which the wide spreading mats choose to grow, of an aversion to any damage sustained by the deep running, wiry roots, and the slowness with which cuttings will root (four months with the little material so far available) helps to form a basis for further research.

The process is not one of universal improvement; on the contrary failure can be more marked than in any other aspect of alpine gardening. But looking back over the number of alpines considered 'impossible' until someone took the trouble to investigate their needs, it is obviously one from which we are all likely to benefit.

A recurrent problem with new introductions is that of identification. Unlike the examples above, it is likely that a proportion of the wild-collected seed that is received will have only the genus – or perhaps the family – against a number on the field notes, since the plant may not have been found in flower. This can be true even of Europe, where one might expect greatest familiarity with the alpine flora; and by the stage that the origin is far flung – southwestern Alaska perhaps, or Soviet Central Asia – at least 50 per cent of the share is likely to be so 'identified'.

In theory, the collector concerned will have made herbarium specimens, or be able to consult past records and marry them against notes taken in the field, contacting subscribers at a later date with the relevant information. In practice he or she is busy planning the next trip, or is otherwise unable to spare the considerable amount of time such researches demand, And so it is often found that the person who raises the stock has to wait until the plant flowers or produces unmistakably unique foliage, whereupon a combination of checking with any existing flora and consulting those familiar with alpine plants of the region concerned might provide a satisfactory identification. The frustration occurs when neither of these approaches bears fruit.

What must be emphasised is that any information provided by the collector should be retained. The number used to identify the particular plant should be written on the label and, for preference, entered into a stock book with the source, date of sowing, name of plant if given (but keep an open mind; mistakes do occur, and seed is sometimes inadvertently mixed) and, where feasible, number of seeds sown. The same species may have been collected in three separate sites: *do not* amalgamate the packets, whether each contains just a few seeds or not, because they may well differ markedly from one population to another.

Some people agonise about what compost to use, but the altitude at which the plant was found, coupled with the minimum description of its habitat (scree, rockface, meadow, woodland) should be sufficient. If absolutely nothing is known, then an ordinary potting compost (omitting any added fertiliser) should be used: seedlings that object to this in their early stages are unlikely to adapt to any conditions that could be provided. The standard rule of 'the higher the alpine, the greater the drainage required' is not foolproof, but still has much to commend it.

It is surprising how many alpines have remained in cultivation from just one introduction, and also the number that can be traced back to one seedling. Given an identical batch of material, the difference in stock raised between one gardener and another, supposedly using the same methods, are usually appreciable.

To conclude, one might include a plea that anyone receiving unfamilar material should attempt to propagate it as soon as possible, and then conduct trials to see how best to grow the stock raised. Instead of potting up the young plants at the same time, in the same compost and placing them in a common block try one or two different sites, experiment with slow release fertilisers and frequency of replanting, recording the variation in the results.

107

Summary dry habitats

The chief purpose of an alpine house is usually perceived as being to protect its occupants from winter wet. By no means can all the plants be left in open plunge beds once they have finished flowering, however. Quite a number are intolerant of moisture lodging in their crowns and keeping the compost damp – with some, harsh and drying winds make short work of any rainfall that might be experienced in the wild. Others grow in positions where moisture is soon shed from the foliage, and yet others simply go dormant as soon as the spring snowmelt rainfall dies away, only restarting growth with the trigger of cooler autumn temperatures.

The last group is perhaps the least understood. When the rugged mound loses all vitality except in the tip of the shoots, and the cladding leaves turn lifeless, it is difficult to appreciate that this may simply be normal behaviour. And yet I found that photographs of *Phlox bryoides* taken only a few weeks after the mounds of imbricated, silvery foliage were peppered with small white flowers, show scorched looking hummocks, presumably with their extensive roots reaching down several metres into barely moist strata in a way they cannot if confined within a pot. This is a plant that has the reputation of being reluctant to flower regularly under alpine house conditions: the 'heat treatment' might be implicated, but in Nevada and Montana the mature cushions do not always flower, depending on the generosity of the previous year's display and the moisture level of the soil at the time of bud formation.

It is well known that the foliage commonly indicates the nature of the climate which the plant experiences. Densely hairy foliage is one such adaptation, as are thick and fleshy leaves, which resist desiccation and the intense insolation to which they may be subjected. Such plants generally have a noticeably thickened rootstock known as a caudex, which can extend some considerable depth into the growing medium, passing imperceptibly from aerial stem to taproot. This is rather different from those species where new roots are formed annually, and is a feature of plants that are restricted to well-drained soils, because any waterlogging will cause an oxygen deficiency that can soon lead to substantial root damage.

The aforementioned genus *Lewisia* epitomises this adaptation, and whilst some of the species can be grown outside in vertical crevices or sites where water does not collect on the soil surface, when the crowns build up the danger of moisture becoming trapped at the leaf bases increases, and old plants are usually happy with glass protection. In high summer, when the deciduous species have retired underground, those that remain in leaf are able to withstand high temperatures by in effect 'shutting down', ceasing vegetative growth, and perhaps allowing the outer leaves to shrivel and incurve. A bare minimum of water provided by the damp plunge material, is all that is needed. Much the same is true of the closely related plant, *Claytonia megarhiza* v. *nivalis* which grows easily under glass, very slowly building up its crowns of thick, spoon-shaped leaves and, when covered by racemes of rose pink flowers, living up to its common name of Alpine Spring Beauty. Propagation can be achieved by detaching rosettes in late spring with a sharp knife or razor blade, whence they root quite easily in slightly damp silver sand on the open bench, but seed-raised plants generally seem to grow more readily.

A similar adaptation is seen in the rosulate violas of Chile and Argentina. Depending on the species, they are capable of forming succulent mounds up to 40cm across, although more usually one finds single rosettes on the windswept gravel terraces or vast sweeping screes. So far few are thought to have been brought much beyond their first flowering, and an added complication is the apparent etiolation of the root stock. At least 30 species are known, frequently localised in their distribution; none except *Viola cotyledon*, with its circlets of pink or mauve-coloured flowers, carried close to the toughened leaves, has any garden history at all. Seed is still rarely available, and whilst it can germinate reasonably well, it has been the general experience that overwatering soon despatches the young plants. The draughtiest, sunniest spot in the alpine house is required if the plants are to remain reasonably compact, but the initial lengthening of the hypocotyl is a feature of the plant in the wild too, and a satisfactory response is to repot progressively deeper, filling the distance between the roots and the (usually) columnar rosette with coarse chippings or rock fragments.

What can surprise anyone unfamiliar with the behaviour of alpines from the warmer regions is the speed with which they appear above ground, flower and retire. The whole event can in some cases be telescoped into a period of a month. Several of the northwest American species of viola with dissected leaves behave in this fashion, their rootstocks travelling far underground and utilising the spring rains before the soil dries out. None are offered on a commercial basis, but seed of bicoloured *Viola beckwithii* and the rather similar *V. trinervata* has given rise to a few plants at one time or another, and one sees rarely the yellow *V. douglasii*, found in a variety of locations through Oregon and California, but suspiciously short-lived in cultivation. After their spring flowering, no further water need be given until the late autumn, when a cautious watering will revitalise the root system.

The behaviour is very much akin to many bulbous plants, of which the alpine house owner has a vast range to choose from, not all of them strictly requiring glass protection. The most appropriate ones grow in regions that experience a mediterranean-type climate, each country subjected to a variation on the theme of warm/hot summers with little if any rainfall, and winters that can be marked by heavy rain. The mountainous areas surrounding the Mediterranean itself and the Anatolian plateau leading on into central Asia, have long provided us with the majority of suitable bulbs, although other areas of the world – particularly South Africa and California – are home to some of the finest species the garden can boast. Particularly with the higher altitude species, a cold period is quite in keeping with their normal growth cycle: if the winter is relatively mild, this can be harmful in that it encourages the new shoots to develop, which then become frost damaged and susceptible to frost attack. A further disadvantage manifests itself when flowers open too soon, frequently before the bud has drawn clear of the new leaves. This can be overcome by placing an inverted flower pot over the emerging spike for a few days, which will help to lengthen the stem.

Of all the monocots grown in the alpine house, the most popular genus is probably still *Fritillaria*, not simply because a number of them are conspicuously attractive but equally for the diversity contained and also, perhaps, for the challenge presented by the ones that seldom flower well. Some make first-rate garden plants, whereas others will grow happily in the open for some years, until a markedly damp summer or late frost reduces their numbers. A specialist in the genus *Fritillaria* will always advise you to grow other plants as well, because the erratic flowering of the species whose corms split up if handled carelessly, and the relatively slow period that it takes to achieve a flowering-size plant from seed, mean that anticipating the end result is often half the fun of growing them.

Focusing on the more reliable species, the large chequered yellow bells of Turkish *Fritillaria aurea* are produced annually, and the hundreds of tiny bulbils that form at the base of the corm provide an ideal, if long-winded method of increase. This is a plant of sparse, upland turf (usually on limestone) and responds well to a substantial sprinkling of bonemeal in the compost. A sandy loam has proved suitable, and repotting is carried out in late summer every year, which gives a chance to separate the bulbs and grow them on separately. Once flowering is over, pot-grown specimens can be removed to a glass-covered plunge (some people advocate leaving them uncovered, but in a wet season they suffer from botrytis which usually starts at the base of the stem) and kept in growth for as long as possible, adding a half strength dose of a high potash liquid feed to the contents of the watering can every fortnight or so. Once the leaves die down in early summer, watering ceases for up to three months until the corms are graded in the autumn.

Just a few of the members of the genus seem to appreciate a warm, dry rest, and in some areas can be left on benching unplunged for their summer dormant phase. Having read that *Fritillaria pluriflora* could be found in parched Californian fields, where reaching down into the cracks the bulbs could be lifted easily, I selected this species and suspect it was happier than in a cold frame. *F. pudica* also responded, the oddly sombrero-shaped corms showing none of the discoloration that can affect those that rest in even a barely hand-damp compost, but this does not hold true everywhere. There are endless records of *F. pudica* being planted outside and failing to survive beyond the first season, and also a few from northern Europe of the same species growing happily outside, and the wise gardener will raise enough stock to carry out comparative trials.

Of those widely available species that tend to grow better under glass, one might mention *F. bucharica* with its tall nodding wands of greenish white flowers, *F. graeca* with chocolate brown and green bells, the recently popular and surprisingly manageable *F. stenanthera* and the delicate *F. uva-vulpis*, none of which should present undue difficulties, though the number of flowers produced by some of them reflects the cultural skill brought to bear.

Several of the Turkish species occupy common territory with some of the Oncocyclus group of *Iris*, and here again we have a body of plants that prefer hot, dry summers and do not normally persist for long when outside, even in areas that provide relevant conditions. When happy, they can grow with remarkable ease, and marvellously showy plants such as *Iris iberica* ssp. *elegantissima* find a refuge in the alpine house, though their massive roots and variable height (up to 40cm in cultivation) are not always easily accommodated. In the cooler summers of northern Europe, the post-flowering shoots do not necessarily die down, and the perennial roots continue to grow. This species is a true alpine, found at altitudes of up to 2,000m, but further south in Israel and Jordan species from far more modest heights occur, and can be expected to react adversely to wintertime temperatures that the rest of the alpine house occupants find perfectly acceptable.

Early and late flowering

The spring period normally encompasses the flowering of most plants in the alpine house, but there are a number of interesting species that develop their flowers either very early or especially late in the year. In the open, the inclement weather that can be expected at these times may ruin the flowers before they are fully developed, whereas in the alpine house one can usually enjoy a varied display at an early date. (Greenhouses almost always provide daytime warmth that has a 'forcing' effect.) The exact timing will vary from year to year depending on the severity of the winter. Those plants that have flowers which were well formed the previous autumn will often promote these quite speedily given a mild spell.

A majority of the species that provide early colour are bulbs, and quite a few are surprisingly resilient to low temperatures, although sustained frost when the plants are in full flower can obviously be damaging. One of the first to flower is *Cyclamen coum*, whose rather squat flowers can be had in all shades of pink, with the occasional albino, usually tinged with carmine at the base of each petal. The wide natural distribution of this species is reflected in the cold hardiness of the plants, which varies considerably, with those that can be traced to lowland coastal sites (from northeastern Turkey, for example) often more pronounced in their sensitivity to low temperatures. However, the majority of corms will have been bred from garden stocks and this inheritance equips them for inclement weather. If grown under glass, their leaves can be damaged by strong sunlight, and light shading may be necessary from mid-spring until the leaves die away.

The recently described *Sternbergia candida*, first grown in our gardens in around 1980, departs from the rest of the species both in its white flowers and

111

the regularity with which they are produced. Its need for a warm dry summer and a deep root run return it to the fold.

Appearing as early as late autumn in some years (although more usually from early winter onwards) *Ranunculus calandrinioides* from the Middle Atlas of Morocco can be relied upon to produce a succession of large white flowers tinged with pink, above somewhat waxy glaucous foliage. The width of the petals can differ appreciatively, with those flowers where they overlap generally preferred. At one time this was a frequently grown plant, but nowadays plants are less easily come by. Luckily seed is still offered, and whilst it is preferable if this can be sown fresh, stored stocks will give a less even germination that makes it worth keeping the pot for at least three years if space permits. Once plants are to hand, division of the crowns in autumn, when growth is restarted after a dry summer, is straightforward. It does well if planted out in the alpine house or bulb frame, doubtless appreciating the extra root run, but as with numerous other *Ranunculus*, appears to exhaust the compost quickly.

Another North African species, *Asphodelus acaulis* can be treated similarly, except that the compost should not be too rich, or else the long, narrow leaves will develop apace, growing upright from the crown instead of spreading to reveal the stemless clusters of pale pink, starry flowers, numbering up to a score on a well-grown plant. There is a suspicion that watering too early in the season can have much the same consequence: the leaves then appear in mid-summer, and by flowering time have developed too far. This is perhaps why it is not grown outside more often – in a well-drained soil it is normally hardy, although in severe winters it has been observed to suffer badly.

However, a plant that few people consider attempting in the open is *Iris nicolai*, in cultivation a very dwarf species, which forms several thickened roots topped by scarcely developed leaves at the turn of the year. Usually the flowers, generally cream with an overlay of deep violet and orange markings on the crest, are produced singly, and should be removed as they wither, because coming as it does from the borderlands of Afghanistan and the USSR, damp, still conditions are anathema and tend very quickly to beckon botrytis infection. The variously coloured *I. galatica* and *I. persica* are just as early into bloom, in mild winters flowering soon after Christmas, but clonal increase seems to be rare, and for garden purposes a hybrid of the same section. *I. × sindpers* (the spelling varies), is more dependable. It is advisable to site these plants by the ventilators along the side of the alpine house away from the prevailing wind, which lessens the chance of rain lodging in the new foliage.

More dependable, and quite possible outdoors, *Sisyrinchium douglasii* is sometimes badly damaged by heavy snow and strong winds, whereas in the alpine house, the delicate mauve or pure white bells can develop unspoilt. It has the merits of taking up little space – a ten-year-old plant is unlikely to be more than 15cm across – and coming very easily from seed. With many winter-flowering species, incidentally, hand pollination is helpful in achieving a good quantity of seed, simply because insect activity is at a low ebb. The reed-like

112

foliage develops from a late winter start, the rootstock lying just below the soil surface and tolerant of summer moisture, despite the rainless conditions sometimes experienced by the wild plant.

Few of the primulas can be had in flower before spring, although just one or two clones of *Primula allionii*, notably 'Praecox' and the diminutive 'Pinkie', have an early blooming habit. Turning however to the Petiolarid section, whose distribution is centred in the Himalayas, we find that a number of the subalpine species can be found flowering in the wild as early as mid-autumn, continuing until summer, depending on the species involved and the altitude at which it occurs. Strictly speaking, they are far from suitable as permanent occupants of the alpine house, hating the heat of summer and usually needing the kind of subdued light and moisture levels provided by their often shaded natural locations.

Against this should be balanced the susceptibility of the early-flowering species to frost, and the likelihood that the attractive covering of farina which adorns the new foliage of several species will be blemished by heavy rainfall. The species that best tolerates permanent alpine house residency is the distinctive cream and yellow *Primula aureata*, possibly because it is not one of the woodland species, but a plant restricted to sheltered crevices at reasonably high altitudes in central Nepal.

For an earlier-flowering species, there is still nothing to touch *P. edgeworthii*, one of the first to settle away from its homeland and established not merely in the mauve of the earlier introductions, but now in near-blue and, at the other extreme pink. These, and a superlative white form whose seedlings still carry on the line upwards of 50 years after it first appeared, start into bloom on average in mid-winter, when the large overwintering bud (which should have its surround of last year's head leaves neatly clipped away in late autumn) opens out to provide a foil of heavily farinose leaves, these expanding rapidly in the ensuing months, though not to the cabbage-like proportions of some close relatives. The crown will multiply, but it is unlikely that the plants are particularly long lived, benefiting from division (as soon as flowering is over) at least every other year, when the plants can be taken back into the shaded frames from which they were removed in the Autumn.

Concluding the list of plants that require round-the-year glass protection, one should include *Dionysia denticulata* and *D. janthina* for their oddly precocious mid-winter blooming habit, chosen from among several other contenders because they are spasmodically available through specialist nurserymen. The warning to be watchful when the flowers die lest botrytis settle and spread, which applies to the majority of winter-blooming plants under glasshouse conditions, is underlined with reference to this genus.

The opposite end of the year presents far fewer opportunities to bring colour into the alpine house. Discounting the stray blooms that can usually be found in all but the most inclement years, my choice lies principally with that handful of bulbs that miss the main autumn crop, and are left to face the heavy rains that can follow, and as such are either sodden or browsed away by the rampant slug populations that such conditions promote.

It is to the eastern Mediterranean and Japan that we must principally look when seeking easily available plants that flower during the later autumn. To this list could be added Africa, both north and south, where the few that have so far gained ground augur well for the future.

The autumn-flowering crocus are not grown under glass as widely as some of them deserve to be, and in late autumn clumps of *Crocus goulimyi* and *C. niveus* (despite the name, lavender tinged as well as pure white) can provide quite a spectacle on a sunny day, contemporaneous with their display in the southernmost Peloponnese. Both are slightly unusual in being synanthous (the leaves are present at flowering time) a character shared by *C. tournefortii*, which goes one better by having flowers that once open, remain so whatever the weather.

The theory that this genus had an aversion to being grown in pots has long since been discredited, as has the necessity of annual repotting. What is important is that the corms should be encouraged to build up by additional feeding – E.A. Bowles was one of the first to recognise this, suggesting applications of bonemeal in the early autumn and again in late winter/early spring. Much the same results are achieved by the liquid fertilisers whose usage has increased since then.

A relatively expensive bulb to acquire, but reliable in its constitution if not the exact timing of its blooms, *Galanthus nivalis* ssp. *reginae olgae* can emerge anytime between early autumn and late winter, in most years inclining towards the earlier date. Its novelty value persuades us to bring it in from the open garden, although experiments suggest a dislike of cool damp summers, with increase in stocks more reliable in the alpine house.

The genus *Allium* is one that the gardener tends to approach rather warily, mindful of the invasive members that form bulbils in the inflorescence or seed abundantly. This reservation should not deter anyone attempting *A. virguncu-lae* from southern Japan, a virtual evergreen in conformity with the year-round precipitation and kinder climate of this latitude. The umbels of small, starry pink flowers, held erect, are freely produced and very showy: no special treatment is required, but obviously the compost should not be allowed to dry out in the summer. Seed is gradually becoming available of another autumn-flowering species that responds well to a drier summer, *A. thunbergii*, with slightly pendent, much darker coloured and well-shaped flowers, the exserted stamens contributing to an appropriately Oriental appearance.

Japan also provides several autumn-blooming saxifrages of the Irregulares section, characterised by their airy panicles of wispy blooms, in which one or perhaps two of the lower petals are at least twice the length of the rest, giving the impression of a narrow lip. For the alpine house, the approximately named dwarf forms of *Saxifraga fortunei* ('Nana', 'Pymaea Rubrifolia', Mt Nachi' and the rest) are ideal, seldom more than 10cm high and retaining their pure white flowers for weeks upon end if an inverted terracotta pot protects them when severe frost is forecast. The leaves, less glossy in these minature forms, can be any colour from mid-green to dark cherry red, usually deeply toothed and an attraction in themselves. In some years the plant will come through unscathed in a shaded part of the peat garden, which gives an indication of the compost and amount of watering preferred.

There are several autumn blooming *Narcissus*, but apart from the one already mentioned (p. 93) their erratic flowering when cultivated confines their appeal to the single-minded specialist. Advice to give them a dry, warm summer rest and allow the bulbs to multiply undisturbed echoes that applied to another member of the Amaryllidaceae, the South African Nerine. Again it is a question of selecting the smaller dwarf species – there are several, those found far inland on the mountain slopes having a good record of cold hardiness. The flowering time is closely linked, it would seem, to the first watering that interrupts their dormancy. This is understandable in relation to *Nerine filifolia*, distributed as far as the fringes of the Kalahari, and presumably triggered into growth whenever the rains come, this accounting for a flowering period spread out over six months from mid-winter until summer. In England, the heads of up to twelve rosy pink flowers, their sepals crinkled in the distinctive manner of the genus, are at their best from late October, an initial watering having taken place in August.

Many of the best *Oxalis* are summer flowering and originate in South America, but species from the other side of the Atlantic are becoming increasingly popular. The one to mention here is *Oxalis hirta*, a vigorous plant once established, with unusually upright growths, the pink flowers suspended on long pedicels that arise from axils along the upper half of the main stems. No water need be given until the first bristly shoots emerge from their summer dormancy, and the lime-free compost is then kept just moist to the touch (but certainly not wet) until mid-spring, when the by then rather untidy foliage dies down. It has tolerated frosts down to $-10°C$ but is regarded with some suspicion on this score, consigned to that somewhat maligned category of alpines that are labelled frost tender.

Resilience to low temperatures

If mountains were all of the temperate, snow-capped peak variety, if alpines did not extend their range beyond the upper reaches of such territory, and if lowland winters did not vacillate treacherously from week to week, never mind year to year, it is doubtful that we would hear very much about cold hardiness, and more specifically the lack of it, in the plants we choose to grow. We would have to forget about the damaging effects of cold weather seen in vegetation at alpine levels, about the well-documented way in which shoots not covered by the snow can be literally abraded by sleet, and the distinct selectivity of some plants where an overhanging bank or slight hollow makes all the difference between a healthy seedling and a dead one, but we woud have a satisfying means of deciding what not to include in an alpine house.

Inconveniently, mountains occur at a variety of latitudes and differ greatly in character. Some never lose an upper covering of snow, others do not even receive a light dusting depending on the season. Their plants, a few of them anyway, are to be found beyond the lower slopes, which of course is the thin end of the wedge, leading as it does to the plants that grow with them in these locations, or indeed species in the same genus that appear to be of horticultural interest.

Kept in check, this is no bad thing, but when the stage is reached where most of the dwarf plants grown are those confined to rocky coastlines, prairies, desert fringes, low sierras and subalpine woodlands, the overall collection could scarcely be considered alpine. Limiting the selection to those plants found exclusively or regularly at the upper limit of their distribution on a mountain (defined in the dictionary as a 'large or high and steep hill, especially one over 1,000m') is a useful starting point, but still lets in exotic orchids such as *Vanda* – found at up to 2,000m in northern India. So the second criterion admits only those species that grow where temperatures of freezing point or below may be experienced, not necessarily that the plant is regularly subjected to them, depending on the timing and the snow cover available. The third stipulation – an arbitrary one – limits the height of the plant: for alpine houses few of the plants will be more than 30cm tall, the majority much less.

This sifting out process still leaves many plants that cause anxious moments in some winters. For one person they may naturalise out of doors without hesitation – five or ten miles away the same species very likely behaves quite differently, its foliage blackening with the first frost of the season. Glass protection can offer some assistance, but brings its own problems, encouraging early growth which can be damaged when outdoor plants are still dormant and as such more resistant, or encouraging the owner to bring in pots without plunging them, which then freeze solid to the detriment of the incarcerated root.

A fibrous root system is seldom damaged unless the condition is sustained and frost drought occurs, but plants with a thick rhizome, corm or fleshy tuber may be more vulnerable. After a mild winter, the improvement in the condition of many hardy *Cyclamen* is manifest, and though species like *C. repandum* (Plate 11) have been grown in the open over many years, a spot under cover where the sun cannot scorch the thin-textured leaves is appreciated.

The combination of damp and cold constitutes a long-recognised threat for plants at rest, and some plants can simply be dried off and either plunged or completely buried in a dry sand bed under the benching. Failing this, a box of unmoistened peat in an unheated garage will do. This is a surer way of maintaining the central American *Weldenia candida*, never mind the frosts to which it is subjected to in some of its mountainous haunts. Under more favourable conditions, this is an unnecessary precaution. On the covered rock garden at Wisley, where it had a deep root run and the insulation of a generous topdressing of slate fragments, the weldenia grew lustily, increasing its crowns and producing quantities of the pure white, three-petalled blooms.

Presumably the compost retained some moisture, which would suit another supposedly tender plant, *Paeonia cambessedesii*, grown at the back of sheltered borders in the north of England, but rather unwisely recommended as a pot plant, which state it soon outgrows if root disturbance doesn't cause its demise.

The dilemma of how to cope with plants that succumb when planted out, but grow too rapidly under cover, is one known to many alpine house owners. The newly popular Australasian *Hibbertia procumbens* looks set to join this list, for whilst the late spring scattering of rich yellow buttercups, stemless on the open mat, is worth some effort to achieve, the way that the underground stolons explore the surrounding territory needs to be watched. During the summer, water is required in plenty and also light shade, for the strong sun can burn away patches of the topgrowth.

Geranium papuanum, a little-known species from altitudes of up to 3,500m in Papua New Guinea, has a comparable susceptibility – presumably the mist zone effect of its native mountains works against scorching, but why it should be affected by frost (which it undoubtedly encounters at home) is puzzling. In the alpine house it has grown well in areas of slight shade, the runners rooting down in the surrounding pots and soon producing a summer-long succession of purple-pink flowers.

This root-as-you-go habit is a survival strategy that works very much in the gardener's favour. Plants with a single rootstock can be completely killed by some misfortune, but if each small plantlet is an independently functioning satellite, it becomes more likely that one or two of the outer portions will survive, even if the main area perishes. The highly distinctive *Sarmienta repens* does just this, or at least would if grown on a covered peat bank or similar rather than kept in a pot, where the roots which form at the nodes in high summer have nothing to root into. Cuttings root surely but very slowly, and it is doubtless because seedlings are being grown in quantity that we now see this brilliant red Gesneriad adorning more and more alpine houses. Using a seed compost with a high proportion of sphagnum moss is a decided advantage, retaining moisture and not compacting when saturated. A lime-free peaty compost is advisable, and may well influence the colour of the flowers, which in some instances can be a less attractive muddy pink. Its frost tenderness has been overemphasised because of its exotic appearance.

Broken off pieces will root quite well, but not with the alacrity long recognised in the numerous species of *Sedum*. It is not necessary to retain many of them in the alpine house, but the Mexican *S. humifusum* is an exception, disliking both the cold and wet of the north European winter, but covering itself in mid-spring with an abundance of bronze or bright yellow flowers. A 50 per cent John Innes No. 2, 50 per cent grit compost is suitable, working some extra silver sand into the upper layers.

Where a species has a wide altitudinal range, the difference in behaviour of introductions originating from its upper and lower limits can sometimes be exploited by the gardener seeking hardier material. Much can be learned from cultivating stocks of known wild origin from a variety of locations, for some will adapt much better than others to their changed environment, quite apart from the differences in actual appearance that one could expect to find.

Species with a highly diverse distribution – *Parrya nudicaulis* from Alaska, a few sites in the Rockies, Siberia, the Karakorams and parts of the Himalayas being a good example – may retain the behaviour specific to their individual race when cultivated, and as a subdivision a vertical separation of just a few hundred metres can be critical when cold tolerance is a consideration.

One of the most distinctive autumn-flowering gentians, *Gentiana depressa*, which after years of near extinction as a garden plant has made a reasonable comeback, is well known for its susceptibility to frost drought. It is probable that the species is chiefly represented by just one or two Nepalese collections, and one wonders if seed from further east, or even from its upper altitudinal limit, would lead to stock that remained unaffected by the problem. Such a varying response is familiar in a number of Himalayan plants – *Fritillaria cirrhosa*, *Meconopsis horridula* and *Rhododendron lepidotum* come readily to mind – and is undoubtedly true of a great many other species. It is simply that we have not had the chance to grow them side by side and assess their behaviour.

Intolerance of winter damp

When at rest, the majority of alpines are best grown in such a way that water drains efficiently through the growing medium. If grown in even a modestly raised site that cannot become waterlogged, they may tolerate winter rainfall levels that do not occur in their wild state, usually because any precipitation comes in the form of snow.

Efficient drainage, however, is not enough. The topgrowth becomes matted through constant soaking, and the lower evaporation rates prevalent mean that for days or weeks on end the persistent dead leaves hold moisture around the vulnerable dormant shoots. Plants equipped to withstand the desiccating effects of much drier climates show characteristic adaptations of the leaf surface, which is commonly obscured by a dense covering of hairs – something that works against them in a damper environment.

Relatively few gardeners can provide conditions of guaranteed snow cover, and the very approximate alternative is to cover the plants with some form of shield, though open at the sides to encourage good ventilation. In the rock garden, panes of glass propped up against bricks or suspended above on a wire framework can be very useful, but the effort involved discourages widespread usage, and in a gale only the most securely bolted down covers will stay in place. Seen this way, the alpine house is simply a more systematic way of gathering together plants that are better grown with their topgrowth kept dry over the winter months (though most will require that their compost does not dry out completely).

It is not quite enough to shield the plants from rainfall and check the soundness of the structure to prevent water dripping down onto the plants. Fog and mist will pose the threat of water droplets condensing on the plants and inner framework. An extractor fan can be a great help when such conditions prevail. If overcast and still weather follows, making it likely that normal ventilation will not disperse the excess moisture, it is worth hunting out a roll of paper kitchen towel, and carefully patting the sheets against the topgrowth to absorb any dampness. At the same time, wiping down the interior faces of the glazing not only removes further moisture but in the process improves light transmission by clearing dust deposits that may have built up.

Virtually all of the plants mentioned so far will benefit if so treated. For species that come from summer dry habitats, such treatment is probably advisable the year round. The roots will not necessarily dry out, especially at the highest altitudes where the three-month (or less) summer means that snow melt has a moderating effect, but negligible rainfall and the sheltered positions often chosen explain an intolerance of overhead moisture. Plants that retain their foliage and grow on the open slopes in such regions tend to have harsh, resilient foliage – *Acantholimon* from the Eurasian steppe for instance – and in a well-drained position can tolerate open garden conditions whereas those with densely felted, generally soft leaves object strongly. If found growing in open conditions, then they adapt to the heat and drought by retiring to resting buds, storing their water needs by means of succulent leaves, extending their root system very considerably and utilising a wind-resistant growth habit.

One growth form not restricted to these areas, but highly characteristic of upper alpine levels in the build up of a densely packed mound of small rosettes, has given rise to the term 'cushion plant'. Generally they are based on a single rootstock that branches either in a vertical arrangement, leading to a hemispherical cushion, or horizontally to fashion a mat, but this radial branching pattern is occasionally abandoned if the cushion is surface rooting or increases by underground stolons which merge to form a compact crown of foliage.

Work carried out back in 1914 by Hauri and Schrote identified 26 plant families where typical cushion plants could be found, emphasising their preponderance in the Andes, Tasmania and New Zealand Alps, but suggesting that a quarter of those known came from the Himalayas, central Asia and Turkey. They epitomise the reduction in leaf area and adaptation to severe climate that we look for in alpine plants, occurring where more vigorous vegetation starts to peter out and enduring, sometimes in quite dense stands but classically as isolated plants welling from vertical rock crevices or stabilised scree, to altitudes of over 6,000m (*Stellaria decumbens* and *Arenaria bryophylla* in the Himalayas) – the maximum recorded for any alpine plant.

Interest in growing these plants has become a cult in itself, and the difficulties inherent in persuading them to retain their natural form have been met principally by the alpine house grower. This is not to say that a number will not grow as well – and on occasion a great deal better – in the open. Those that have toughened, glabrous or scleromorphic foliage seldom have any need of glass protection, and in an open position condense their growth in a manner not readily achieved in the glasshouse. *Gypsophila aretioides*, despite its origins in Iran, the Caucasus and the Pamirs, grows reasonably outside, and despite a long-standing reluctance to flower in lowland gardens is one of the automatic choices for people wishing to grow this type of plant.

It is just one example of a plant whose tolerance of other climates surprises, in the same way that it is misleading to refer to the needs of a given genus, when the species within it often behave very differently. Another popular cushion plant, *Draba bryoides imbricata*, is much better planted in an open scree or trough, despite its provenance high in the central Caucasus, whereas *D. longisiliqua*, from the same range of mountains but a cliff-dwelling plant with leaves made silvery-grey by the adpressed hairs, is far better protected by glass the year round.

Without knowing the plant concerned, it is usually possible to make an educated guess on its likely needs merely by examining the leaves. Those with the thickest covering of hair – to the point where the individual form of leaf is masked – nearly always prove the most exacting to grow satisfactorily. Compare the North American *Eriogonum torreyanum* and *E. umbellatum* (whose leaves are dark green on their upper surface) which settle and spread to survive even damp winters, whereas the more highly developed species such as *E. acaule* from Wyoming and *E. shockleyi* (a plant of exposed ridges with especially woolly foliage to combat the dryness) are unable to cope with similar conditions. They and the better-known *E. ovalifolium* have been grown in raised scree beds in the drier, eastern areas of England, but too wet a summer can quickly cause their decline.

Similarly adapted, but requiring a great deal more moisture in the growing season, are the New Zealand plants whose woolly, mounded appearance has given them the descriptive name of 'vegetable sheep' – several species of *Raoulia* and one of *Haastia* (*H. pulvinaris*) are involved. One should perhaps mention that the high rainfall totals for Fiordland do not apply further north east in the mountains of the Craigieburn Range and on into Nelson where these plants occur on exposed, windswept mountain shoulders, often in spots that are emphatically well drained. The temperature may vary 20°C or more between the warmth of midday in high summer and night-time frost – a climatic turnaround repeated in the southern Andes, where studies show that snow can fall in any month of the year.

In the alpine house, these plants are generally grown in a very gritty, lime-free compost, topdressed to a depth (with older plants) of 3–4cm of impermeable rock chippings or gravel, and kept in an unshaded position next to the ventilators. Because they will not have the root reserves of a wild plant, nor the thorough breezes and cold nights that temper the heat of the sun, it is important not to let the compost dry out. The scarcity of mature plants of species like *Raoulia eximia* and *Haastia pulvinaris* in our gardens is testimony to the difficulty of satisfying these requirements.

If a suitable method can be arrived at, then they are immensely longlived, a feature of several such plants where regeneration from seed is uncertain and slow, since it enables the species to survive in unfavourable years. This appears to apply to *Kelseya uniflora*, known from a few sites in the Rocky Mountains (invariably on limestone cliffs) which, on those rare occasions when seed is offered, builds up very slowly into a well-tempered, dense mound of greenish-green rosettes, covered in fine hairs and, in early spring, spangled with invididually insignificant pink flowers. Like the majority of cushion plants that are normally found in vertical crevices, it is best to mimick this habit as far as possible, either by fashioning an artificial crevice in the rockwork or making sure that repotting is left until the roots are coming strongly through the drainage hole, potting just one size up at a time.

The best plan with any plant whose tolerance of winter wet is in doubt is to attempt to propagate it in time for material to be established in the springtime, then be ready to note how it behaves as the end of the year draws in. There is never enough space in an alpine house, and such experiments are an important means of relieving congestion.

Appendix I Societies

There are a number of societies dealing specifically with the cultivation of alpine plants, and several others devoted to a genus, many of whose representatives fall under this general heading. Nearly all of them run an annual seed exchange and produce a journal or yearbook. The majority also conduct a series of shows (The Alpine Garden Society, for example, currently holds 18 across England between March and October) or stage periodic exhibits at more generalised horticultural events such as those arranged by the Royal Horticultural Society.

The list that follows is not intended to be exhaustive, but suggests some of the more appropriate choices, whilst acknowledging the importance of specialist organisation elsewhere, notably the Prague Rock Garden Club and the Japanese Alpine Garden Society.

Alpine Garden Society (AGS)
Secretary: E. M. Upward,
Lye End Link, St John's, Woking,
Surrey GU21 1SW, England

Alpine Club of British Columbia
Membership Chairman: Denys Lloyd,
3281 W. 35th Avenue, Vancouver VN
ZM9, British Columbia

American Rock Garden Society
(ARGS)
Contact: Buffy Parker,
15 Fairmead Road, Darien,
Connecticut 06820 USA.

Botanical Society of South Africa
Contact: The Secretary,
Botanical Society of South Africa,
Claremont 7735, Cape, RSA

Cyclamen Society
Contact: P. Moore,

Tile Barn House, Standen Street,
Iden Green, Benenden, Kent TN17
4LB, England.

New Zealand Alpine Garden
Society
Membership Secretary: Mrs A.
Lemmon,
17 Courage Road, Amberley, New
Zealand.

Saxifraga Group
Secretary: B. Arundel,
3 Pinewood Gardens, Hemel
Hempstead, Herts HP1 1TN,
England.

Scottish Rock Garden Club
(SRGC)
Subscription Secretary: Miss K. M.
Gibb,
21 Merchiston Park, Edinburgh
EH10 4PW, Scotland.

Appendix II Specialist Sources

Relatively few nurseries specialise in plants for the alpine house. But despite fears to the contrary, prompted by the difficulties relating to their propagation and additional time often taken to produce a saleable plant, an ever-widening range of suitable species is offered for sale. Tracking them down to their disparate sources can be a lengthy business, notwithstanding the emergence of directories such as *The Plant Finder*, since the rarer species are not always catalogued, and it is a question of making speculative enquiries.

The following list gives an indication of some established sources, but new nurseries are continually springing up. Not all are able to export, nor even to send their plants through the post, which is where the seed merchants score. From such sources a vast range of material, some of it never satisfactorily established in cultivation, becomes available to enthusiasts, who may not necessarily live in countries where the cultivation of alpine plants has developed sufficiently to see the opening of specialist nurseries.

In addition, there are 'one-off' seed collections made by individuals or small parties who may sell shares and can be contacted by scanning the advertisement section of specialist society journals.

As contacts build up and the collection is established, exchange of material between one gardener and another, quite frequently on an international basis, is likely to be of greater significance. Subject to the constraints governing the removal of plants from the wild, modest introductions from this source can be established and, it is to be hoped, distributed to other interested parties.

Alpine plant nurseries (UK)

Those that specialise in alpine house plants are marked with an asterisk.

* R. F. Beeston, 294 Ombersley Road, Worcester WR3 7HD.

Blackthorn Nursery, Kilmeston, Alresford, Hants SO24 0NL. (*Daphne*, personal callers only.)

Broadleigh Gardens, Barr House, Bishop's Hull, Taunton, Somerset TA4 1AE (Hardy bulbs.)

Butterfields Nursery, Harvest Hill, Bourne End, Bucks SL8 5JJ. (*Pleione*.)

* Cambridge Bulbs (C. F. and N. J. Stevens), 40 Whittlesford Road, Newton, Cambridge CB2 5PA. (*Crocus, Fritillaria, Iris.*)

* P. & J. Christian, Pentre Cottages, Minera, Wrexham, Clwyd LL11 3DP N. Wales. (*Crocus, Corydalis, Fritillaria, Tulipa.*)

K. W. Davis, Brook House, Lingen, Nr Bucknell, Craven Arms, Shropshire SY7 0DY.

Jack Drake, Inshriach Alpine Plant Nursery, Aviemore, Invernessshire PH22 1QS Scotland.

Edrom Nurseries (Propr J. Jermyn), Coldingham, Eyemouth, Berwickshire TD14 5TZ Scotland.

Highgates Alpines (R. E. and D. I. Straughan), 166A Crich Lane, Belper, Derbyshire DE5 1EP. (Personal callers only.)

Holden Clough Nursery (P. J. Foley), Holden, Bolton-by-Bowland, Clitheroe, Lancs BB7 4PF.

W. E. Th. Ingwersen Ltd, Birch Farm Nursery, Gravetye, E. Grinstead, W. Sussex RH19 4LE. 01342 810236

* L. Kreeger, 91 Newton Wood Road, Ashtead, Surrey KT21 1NN. (Also issues a seed list.)

Potterton & Martin, The Cottage Nursery, Moortown Road, Nettleton, Nr Caistor, N. Lincolnshire LN7 6HX.

M. Salmon, Monocot Seeds, Jacklands Bridge, Twickenham, Avon BS21 6SG. (Bulbous plants, seed list.)

D. Sampson, Oakdene Nursery, Scotsford Road, Broadoak, Heathfield, E. Sussex TN21 8TU.

Tile Barn Nursery, Standen Street, Eden Green, Benenden, Kent TN17 4LB. (*Cyclamen.*)

Waterperry Horticultural Centre, Alpine Dept, Nr Wheatley, Oxon OX9 1JL. (*Saxifraga.*)

Commercial seed lists

Jim and Jenny Archibald, 'Bryn Collen', Ffostrasol, Llandysul, Dyfed SA44 5SN, Wales. (Field collected seed – Europe, Turkey, Northwest USA – also from cultivated stock.)

C. Chadwell, 81 Parlaunt Road, Slough, Berks SL3 8BE. (Himalayan genera.)

Chiltern Seeds, Bortree Style, Ulverston, Cumbria LA12 7PB.

L. Kreeger (see nursery list).

Monocot Seeds (see nursery list).

Northside Seeds, Ludlow House, 12 Kingsley Avenue, Kettering, Northants NN16 9EU.

Rocky Mountain Rare Plants, PO Box 20483, Denver, Colorado 80220-0483, USA.

Southern Seeds, The Vicarage, Sheffield, Canterbury, New Zealand.

D. & A. Wraight, 25 rue Paul Eyschen, L-7317 Steinsel, G. D. Luxembourg. (Seed collected in the Andes.)

Alpine plant suppliers (USA)

Colorado Alpines Inc., PO Box 2708, Avon, CO 81620.

Lamb's Nurseries, E.101 Sharp Avenue, Spokane, Washington 99202.

Mt Tahoma Nursery, 28111-112th Avenue East, Graham, Washington 98338.

Oliver Nurseries Inc., 1159 Bronson Road, Fairfield, CT 06430.

Rice Creek Gardens Inc., 1315 66th Avenue Northeast, Minneapolis, MN 55432.

Rocknoll Nursery, 9210 US 50, Hillsboro, Ohio, UT 45133-8546.

Rocky Mountain Rare Plants, PO Box 20483, Denver, CO 80220-0483.

Russell Graham, 4030 Eagle Crest Road Northwest, Salem, OR 97304.

Siskiyou Rare Plant Nursery, 2825 Cummings Road, Medford, OR 97501.

Appendix III Conversion Tables

cm	inches	cm	inches	cm	inches
1	0.39	8	3.15	40	15.74
2	0.79	9	3.54	50	19.68
3	1.18	10	3.93	60	23.62
4	1.57	15	5.90	70	27.55
5	1.97	20	7.87	80	31.49
6	2.36	25	9.84	90	35.43
7	2.76	30	11.81	100	39.37

m	ft	m	ft	m	ft
100	328	600	1,968	1,500	4,921
200	656	700	2,296	2,000	6,562
300	984	800	2,625	2,500	8,202
400	1,313	900	2,953	3,000	9,842
500	1,640	1,000	3,281	3,500	11,483

ha	acres	ha	acres	ha	acres
1	2.5	10	25	100	247
2	5	25	62	150	370
5	12	50	124	200	494

g	oz	kg	lbs	kg	lbs
1	0.04	1	2.2	6	13.2
2	0.07	2	4.4	7	15.4
3	0.11	3	6.6	8	17.6
4	0.14	4	8.8	9	19.8
5	0.18	5	11.0	10	22.0

°C	°F	°C	°F	°C	°F
0	32	12	54	24	75
2	36	14	57	26	79
4	39	16	61	28	82
6	43	18	64	30	86
8	46	20	68	32	90
10	50	22	72	34	93

Select Bibliography

In addition to the books written on either aspects of glasshouse cultivation or plants suitable for this purpose, there are numerous articles that can be consulted in the journals of the AGS (*Bulletin*), ARGS, and SRGC (known since 1983 as *The Rock Garden*). A few address themselves directly to alpine house construction and cultivation, but in most instances the information provided concerns the plants' behaviour in the wild and in our gardens, and the reader must adapt this advice when attempting to grow them. Back copies are often available – the *Bulletin* has been published on a quarterly basis since 1930 – and can be purchased by members of the relevant society. An address list appears in Appendix I.

Anley, G. (1938) *Alpine House Culture for Amateurs*, Country Life, London

Bacon L. (1973) *Alpines*, David and Charles, Newton Abbot

Brickell, C. D. and Mathew, B. (1976) *Daphne*, Alpine Garden Society, Woking

Buczacki, S. and Harris, R. (1981) *Collins Guide to the Pests, Diseases and Disorders of Garden Plants*, Collins, London

Cartman, J. (1985) *Growing New Zealand Alpine Plants*, Reed Metheun, Auckland

Dryden, K. (1988) *Alpines in Pots*, Alpine Garden Society, Saffron Walden

Elliott, J. G. (1970) *Bulbs under Glass*, Alpine Garden Society, London

Elliott, R. C. (1969) *Alpines in Pots*, Alpine Garden Society, London

Fletcher, J. R. (1984) *Diseases in Greenhouse Plants*, Longman Inc., New York

Grey-Wilson, C. (1988) *The Genus Cyclamen*, Christopher Helm, London and Timber Press, Portland

Grey-Wilson, C. (1989) *The Genus Dionysia*, Alpine Garden Society, Woking

Heath, R. E. (1981) *Collectors Alpines*, 2nd edition, Collingridge, London and Timber Press, Portland

Horny, R., Webr, K. and Byam-Grounds, K. (1986) *Porophyllum Saxifrages*, Byam-Grounds, Stamford

Mathew, B. (1982) *The Iris*, Batsford, London and Timber Press, Portland

—— (1988) *The Smaller Bulbs*, Batsford, London

—— (1989) *The Genus Lewisia*, Christopher Helm, London and Timber Press, Portland

Polunin, O. and Stainton, A. (1984) *Flowers of the Himalaya*, Oxford University Press, Oxford

Rix, E. M. (1983) *Growing Bulbs*, Croom Helm, London and Timber Press, Portland

Salmon, J. T. (1968) *Field Guide to the Alpine Plants of New Zealand*, A. H. and A. W. Reed, Wellington

Smith, G. F., Burrow, B. and Lowe, D. B. (1984) *Primulas of Europe and America*, Alpine Garden Society, Woking

Smith, G. F. and Lowe, D. B. (1977) *Androsaces*, Alpine Garden Society, Woking

Stainton, A. (1988) *Flowers of the Himalaya, A Supplement*, Oxford University Press, Oxford

Webb, D. A. and Gornall, R. J. (1989) *Saxifrages of Europe*, Christopher Helm, London and Timber Press, Portland

Willmott, P. K. (1982) *Scientific Greenhouse Gardening*, E. P. Publishing, Wakefield

Woodward, F. I. (1987) *Climate and Plant Distribution*, Cambridge University Press, Cambridge

Index

129